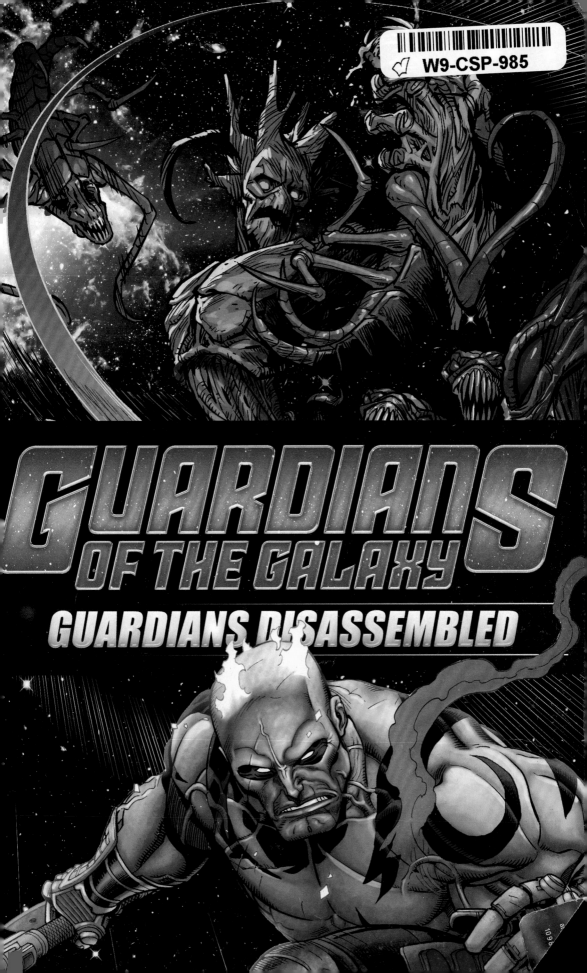

GUARDIANS OF THE GALAXY

GUARDIANS DISASSEMBLED

GUARDIANS
OF THE GALAXY

GUARDIANS DISASSEMBLED

PREVIOUSLY...

PETER QUILL'S ESTRANGED FATHER, THE KING OF SPARTAX, ALONG WITH THE LEADERS OF THE OTHER GALACTIC EMPIRES DECREED THAT NO ALIEN HAND MAY TOUCH THE PLANET EARTH. WHICH THE GUARDIANS PROMPTLY DISOBEYED. THEY HAVE BEEN FUGITIVES EVER SINCE. TO MAKE MATTERS WORSE, A BOUNTY HUNTER, UNDER CONTRACT FROM AN UNKNOWN SOURCE, HAS BEEN HUNTING GAMORA.

THE GUARDIANS RECENTLY MADE ENEMIES OF THE SHI'AR IMPERIAL GUARD AS WELL, WHILE HELPING THE TIME-DISPLACED ORIGINAL X-MEN RESCUE THE YOUNG JEAN GREY FROM THEIR CLUTCHES.

MEANWHILE, THE WARRIOR ANGELA HAS FOUND HERSELF TRANSPLANTED FROM HER OWN UNIVERSE THROUGH SOME ERROR IN THE SPACE-TIME CONTINUUM. UNIDENTIFIABLE AS ANY KNOWN SPECIES, SHE MUST NOW DETERMINE HER PLACE AND PURPOSE IN THE GALAXY.

GUARDIANS OF THE GALAXY VOL. 3: GUARDIANS DISASSEMBLED. Contains material originally published in magazine form as FREE COMIC BOOK DAY 2014 (GUARDIANS OF THE GALAXY) #1, GUARDIANS OF THE GALAXY #14-17, AMAZING SPIDER-MAN #654 and CAPTAIN MARVEL #1. First printing 2015. ISBN# 978-0-7851-8967-1. Published by MARVEL WORLDWIDE, INC., a subsidiary of MARVEL ENTERTAINMENT, LLC. OFFICE OF PUBLICATION: 135 West 50th Street, New York, NY 10020. Copyright © 2015 MARVEL No similarity between any of the names, characters, persons, and/or institutions in this magazine with those of any living or dead person or institution is intended, and any such similarity which may exist is purely coincidental. **Printed in Canada.** ALAN FINE, President, Marvel Entertainment; DAN BUCKLEY, President, TV, Publishing and Brand Management; JOE QUESADA, Chief Creative Officer; TOM BREVOORT, SVP of Publishing; DAVID BOGART, SVP of Operations & Procurement, Publishing; C.B. CEBULSKI, VP of International Development & Brand Management; DAVID GABRIEL, SVP Print, Sales & Marketing; JIM O'KEEFE, VP of Operations & Logistics; DAN CARR, Executive Director of Publishing Technology; SUSAN CRESPI, Editorial Operations Manager; ALEX MORALES, Publishing Operations Manager; STAN LEE, Chairman Emeritus. For information regarding advertising in Marvel Comics or on Marvel.com, please contact Jonathan Rheingold, VP of Custom Solutions & Ad Sales at jrheingold@marvel.com. For Marvel subscription inquiries, please call 800-217-9158. **Manufactured between 5/29/2015 and 7/6/2015 by SOLISCO PRINTERS, SCOTT, QC, CANADA.**

STAR-LORD

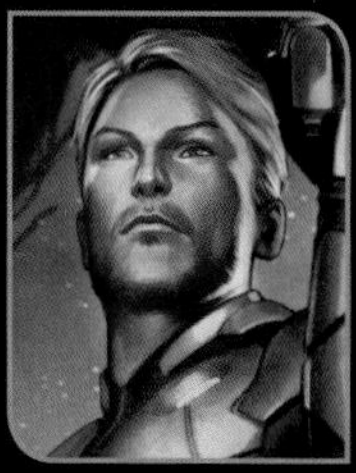

GAMORA

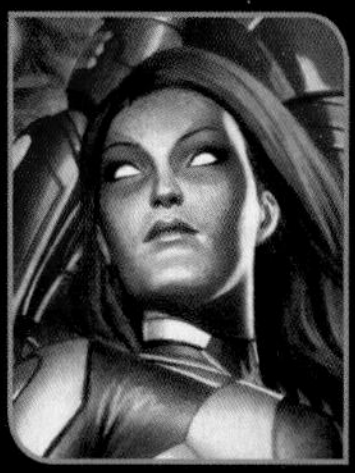

ROCKET RACCOON

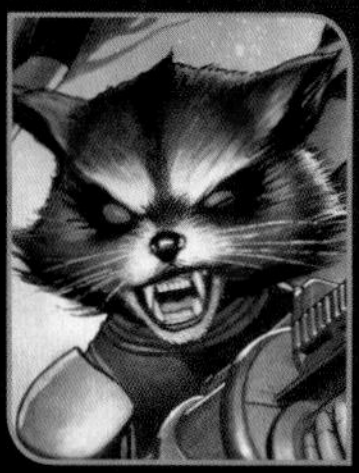

GROOT

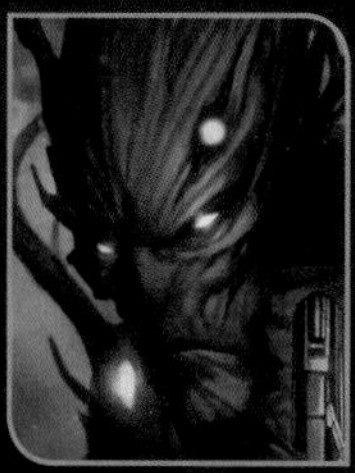

DRAX

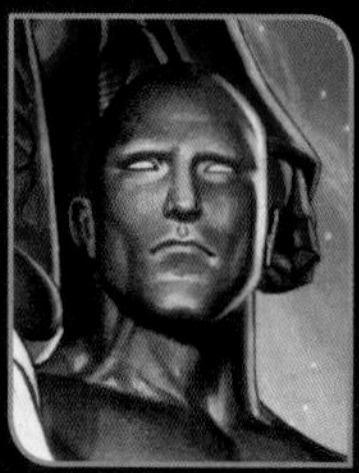

ANGELA

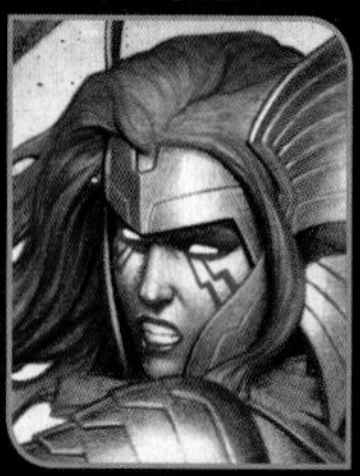

WRITER: **BRIAN MICHAEL BENDIS**

FREE COMIC BOOK DAY 2014 (GUARDIANS OF THE GALAXY) #1
PENCILER: **NICK BRADSHAW**
INKER: **SCOTT HANNA**
COLORIST: **MORRY HOLLOWELL**
LETTERER: **VC'S CORY PETIT**
COVER ART: **SARA PICHELLI & JUSTIN PONSOR**
EDITORS: **STEPHEN WACKER & ELLIE PYLE**

ISSUE #14
ARTISTS: **NICK BRADSHAW WITH JASON MASTERS & TODD NAUCK**
INKERS: **NICK BRADSHAW, WALDEN WONG, JASON MASTERS & TODD NAUCK**
COLORISTS: **JUSTIN PONSOR WITH JASON KEITH**
COVER ART: **NICK BRADSHAW & JUSTIN PONSOR**

"GROOT'S TALE"
WRITER: **ANDY LANNING**
PENCILER: **PHIL JIMENEZ**
INKER: **LIVESAY**
COLORIST: **ANTONIO FABELA**

"FIGHT FOR THE FUTURE"
WRITER: **DAN ABNETT**
ARTIST: **GERARDO SANDOVAL**
COLORIST: **RACHELLE ROSENBERG**

ISSUE #15
PENCILERS: **NICK BRADSHAW & CAMERON STEWART**
INKERS: **NICK BRADSHAW, CAMERON STEWART & WALDEN WONG**
COLORIST: **JUSTIN PONSOR**
COVER ART: **NICK BRADSHAW & JUSTIN PONSOR**

ISSUE #16
ARTISTS: **NICK BRADSHAW, DAVID MARQUEZ & JASON MASTERS**
COLORISTS: **JUSTIN PONSOR, EDGAR DELGADO & JOSE VILLARRUBIA**
COVER ART: **NICK BRADSHAW & JUSTIN PONSOR**

ISSUE #17
PENCILERS: **NICK BRADSHAW & MICHAEL OEMING**
INKERS: **NICK BRADSHAW, MICHAEL OEMING & WALDEN WONG**

COLORIST: **JUSTIN PONSOR**
COVER ART: **ED MCGUINNESS, MARK FARMER & JUSTIN PONSOR**

LETTERER: **VC'S CORY PETIT**
ASSISTANT EDITOR: **XANDER JAROWEY**
EDITOR: **MIKE MARTS**

CAPTAIN MARVEL #1 (2012)
WRITER: **KELLY SUE DECONNICK**
ARTIST: **DEXTER SOY**
LETTERER: **VC'S JOE CARAMAGNA**
COVER ARTISTS: **ED MCGUINNESS, DEXTER VINES & JAVIER RODRIGUEZ**
ASSISTANT EDITOR: **ELLIE PYLE**
EDITOR: **SANA AMANAT**
SENIOR EDITOR: **STEPHEN WACKER**

"REBIRTH" FROM AMAZING SPIDER-MAN #654 (2011)
WRITER: **DAN SLOTT**
PENCILERS: **PAULO SIQUEIRA & RONAN CLIQUET DE OLIVEIRA**
INKERS: **PAULO SIQUEIRA, ROLAND PARIS & GREG ADAMS**
COLORIST: **FABIO D'AURIA**
LETTERER: **VC'S JOE CARAMAGNA**
ASSISTANT EDITOR: **ELLIE PYLE**
SENIOR EDITOR: **STEPHEN WACKER**

COLLECTION EDITOR: JENNIFER GRÜNWALD
ASSISTANT EDITOR: SARAH BRUNSTAD
ASSOCIATE MANAGING EDITOR: ALEX STARBUCK
EDITOR, SPECIAL PROJECTS: MARK D. BEAZLEY
SENIOR EDITOR, SPECIAL PROJECTS: JEFF YOUNGQUIST
SVP PRINT, SALES & MARKETING: DAVID GABRIEL

EDITOR IN CHIEF: AXEL ALONSO
CHIEF CREATIVE OFFICER: JOE QUESADA
PUBLISHER: DAN BUCKLEY
EXECUTIVE PRODUCER: ALAN FINE

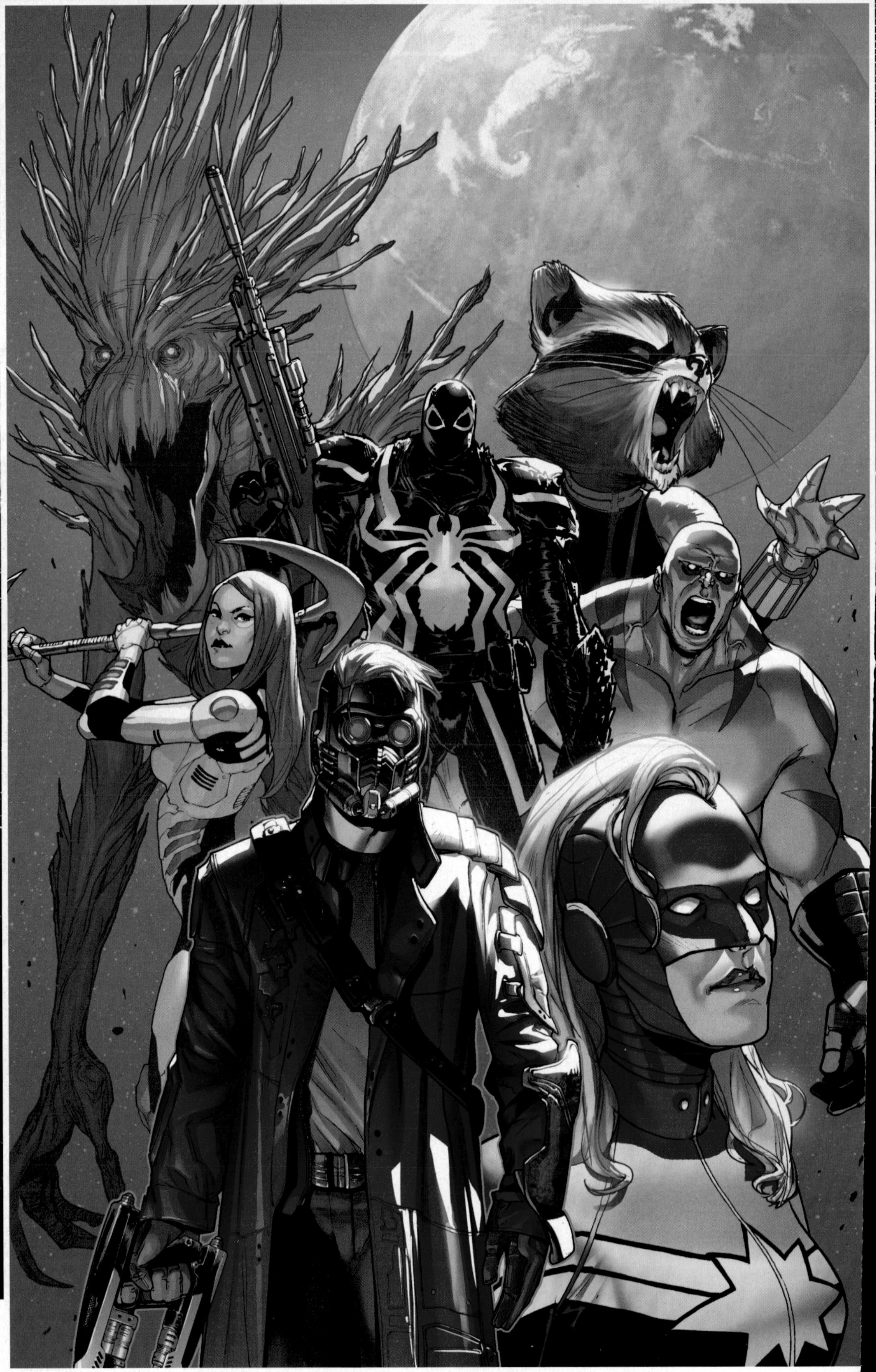

FREE COMIC BOOK DAY 2014 (GUARDIANS OF THE GALAXY) #1

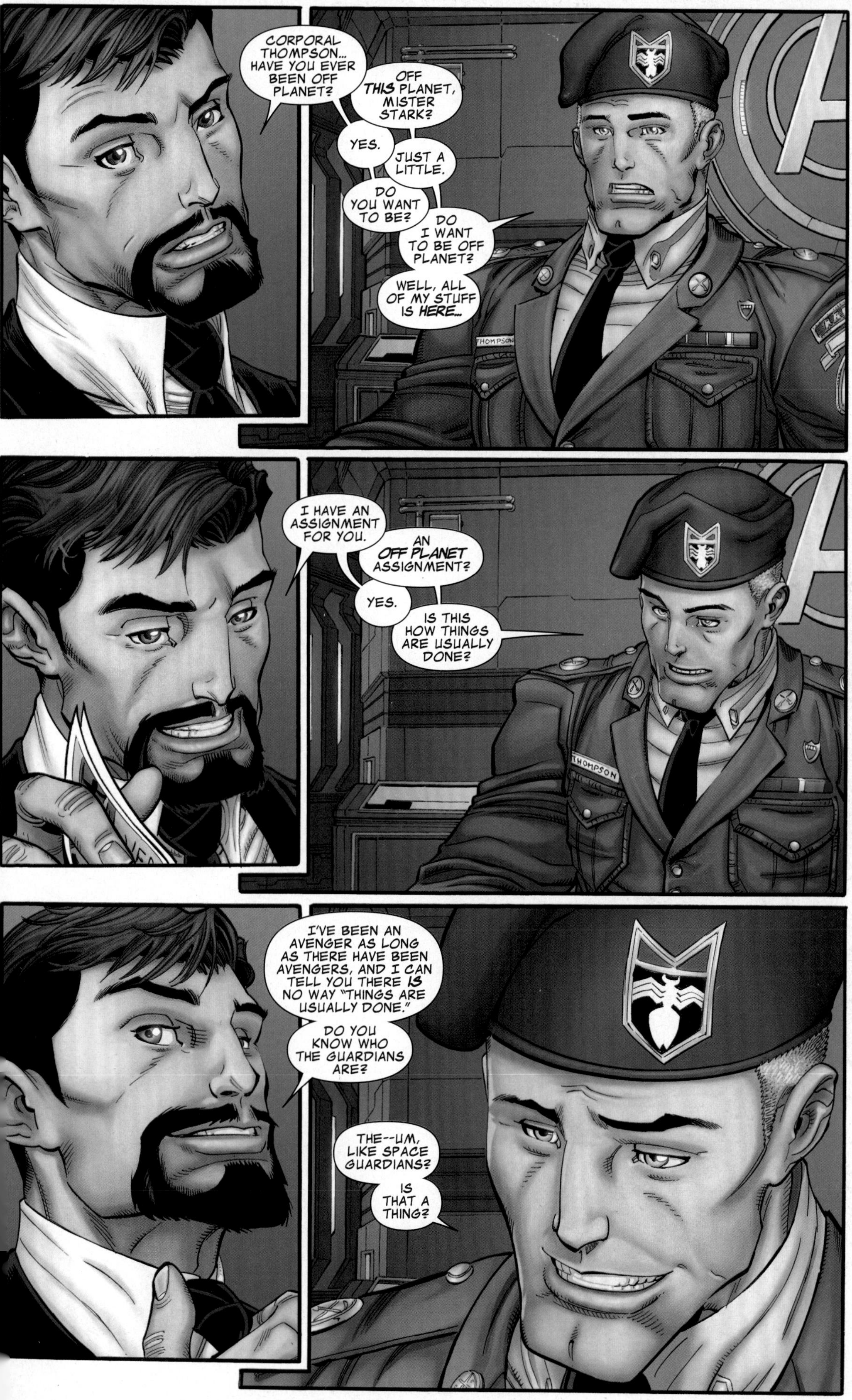
CORPORAL THOMPSON... HAVE YOU EVER BEEN OFF PLANET?
OFF THIS PLANET, MISTER STARK?
YES.
JUST A LITTLE.
DO YOU WANT TO BE?
DO I WANT TO BE OFF PLANET?
WELL, ALL OF MY STUFF IS HERE...
THOMPSON
I HAVE AN ASSIGNMENT FOR YOU.
AN OFF PLANET ASSIGNMENT?
YES.
IS THIS HOW THINGS ARE USUALLY DONE?
THOMPSON
I'VE BEEN AN AVENGER AS LONG AS THERE HAVE BEEN AVENGERS, AND I CAN TELL YOU THERE IS NO WAY "THINGS ARE USUALLY DONE."
DO YOU KNOW WHO THE GUARDIANS ARE?
THE--UM, LIKE SPACE GUARDIANS?
IS THAT A THING?

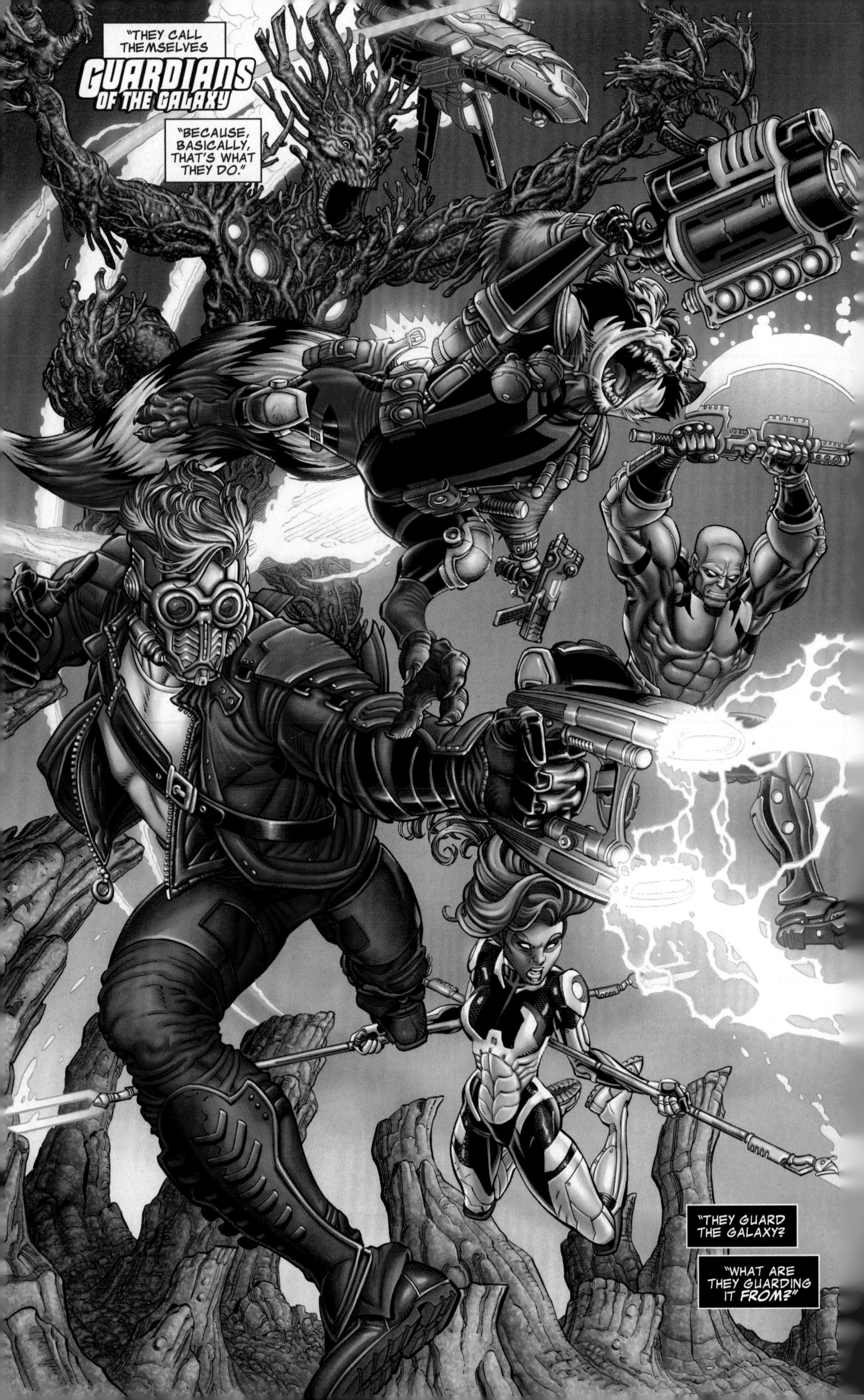
"THEY CALL THEMSELVES
GUARDIANS OF THE GALAXY
"BECAUSE, BASICALLY, THAT'S WHAT THEY DO."
"THEY GUARD THE GALAXY?
"WHAT ARE THEY GUARDING IT FROM?"

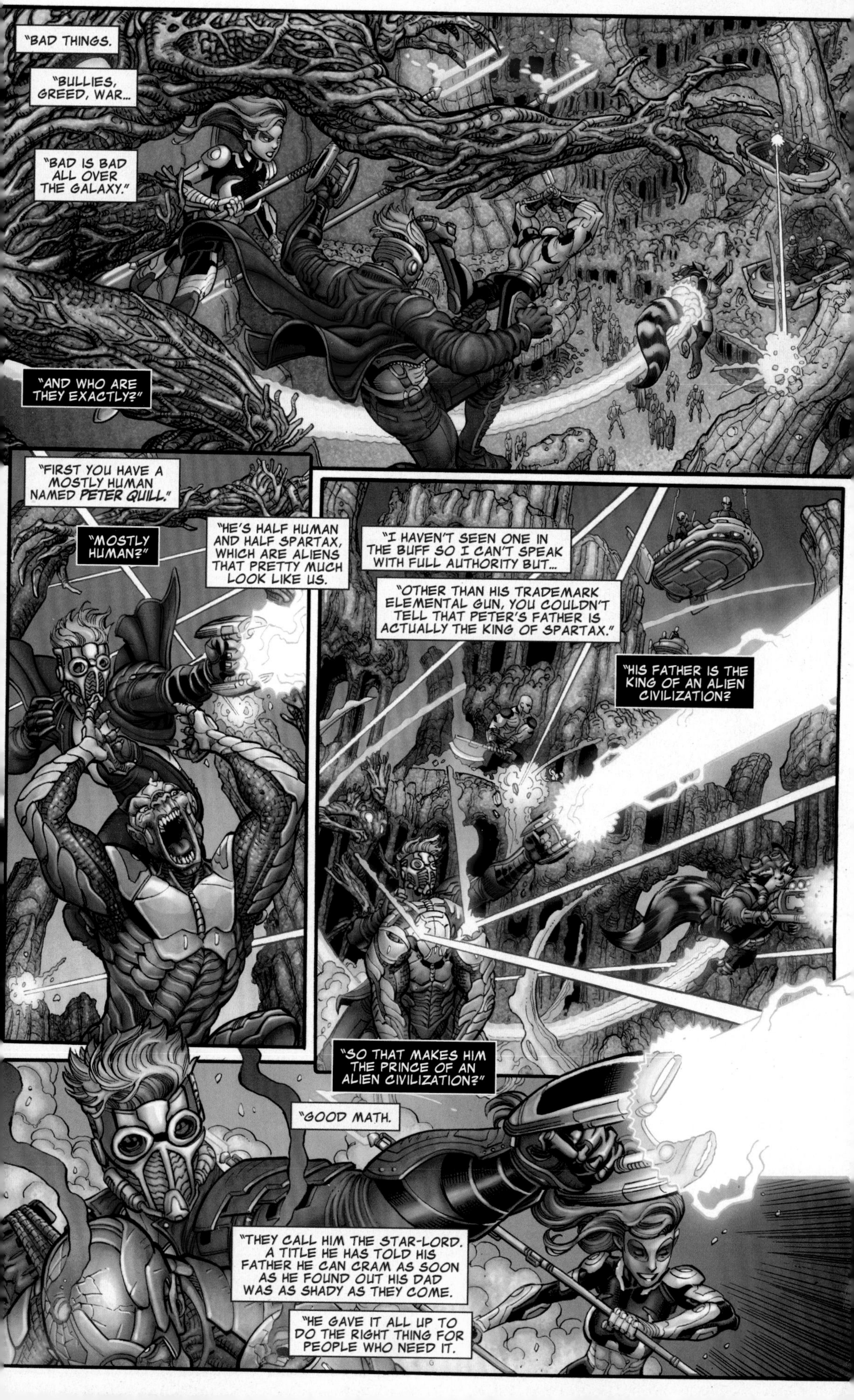
"BAD THINGS.
"BULLIES, GREED, WAR...
"BAD IS BAD ALL OVER THE GALAXY."
"AND WHO ARE THEY EXACTLY?"
"FIRST YOU HAVE A MOSTLY HUMAN NAMED PETER QUILL."
"MOSTLY HUMAN?"
"HE'S HALF HUMAN AND HALF SPARTAX, WHICH ARE ALIENS THAT PRETTY MUCH LOOK LIKE US.
"I HAVEN'T SEEN ONE IN THE BUFF SO I CAN'T SPEAK WITH FULL AUTHORITY BUT...
"OTHER THAN HIS TRADEMARK ELEMENTAL GUN, YOU COULDN'T TELL THAT PETER'S FATHER IS ACTUALLY THE KING OF SPARTAX."
"HIS FATHER IS THE KING OF AN ALIEN CIVILIZATION?
"SO THAT MAKES HIM THE PRINCE OF AN ALIEN CIVILIZATION?"
"GOOD MATH.
"THEY CALL HIM THE STAR-LORD. A TITLE HE HAS TOLD HIS FATHER HE CAN CRAM AS SOON AS HE FOUND OUT HIS DAD WAS AS SHADY AS THEY COME.
"HE GAVE IT ALL UP TO DO THE RIGHT THING FOR PEOPLE WHO NEED IT.

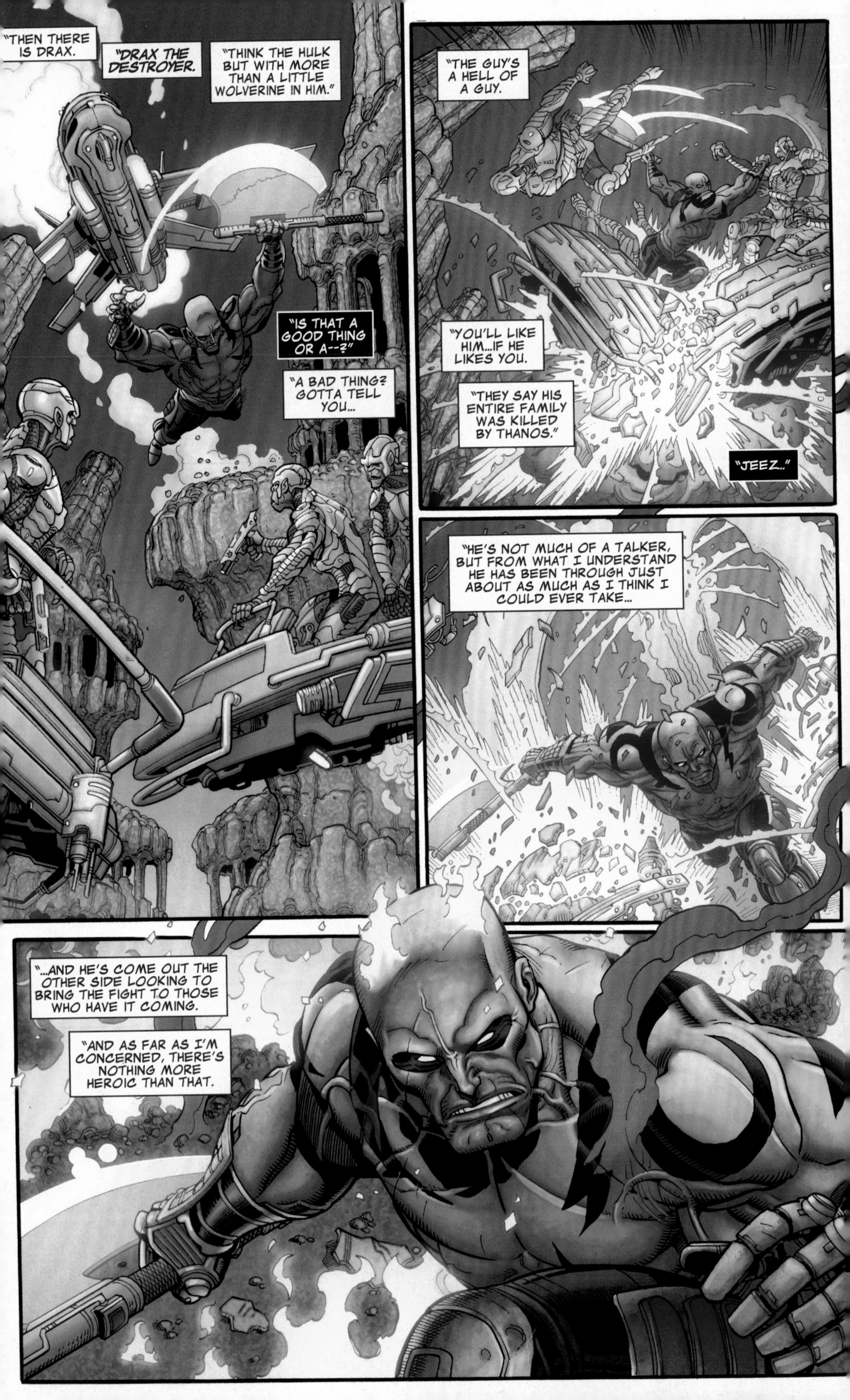
"THEN THERE IS DRAX.
"DRAX THE DESTROYER.
"THINK THE HULK BUT WITH MORE THAN A LITTLE WOLVERINE IN HIM."
"IS THAT A GOOD THING OR A--?"
"A BAD THING? GOTTA TELL YOU...
"THE GUY'S A HELL OF A GUY.
"YOU'LL LIKE HIM...IF HE LIKES YOU.
"THEY SAY HIS ENTIRE FAMILY WAS KILLED BY THANOS."
"JEEZ..."
"HE'S NOT MUCH OF A TALKER, BUT FROM WHAT I UNDERSTAND HE HAS BEEN THROUGH JUST ABOUT AS MUCH AS I THINK I COULD EVER TAKE...
"...AND HE'S COME OUT THE OTHER SIDE LOOKING TO BRING THE FIGHT TO THOSE WHO HAVE IT COMING.
"AND AS FAR AS I'M CONCERNED, THERE'S NOTHING MORE HEROIC THAN THAT.

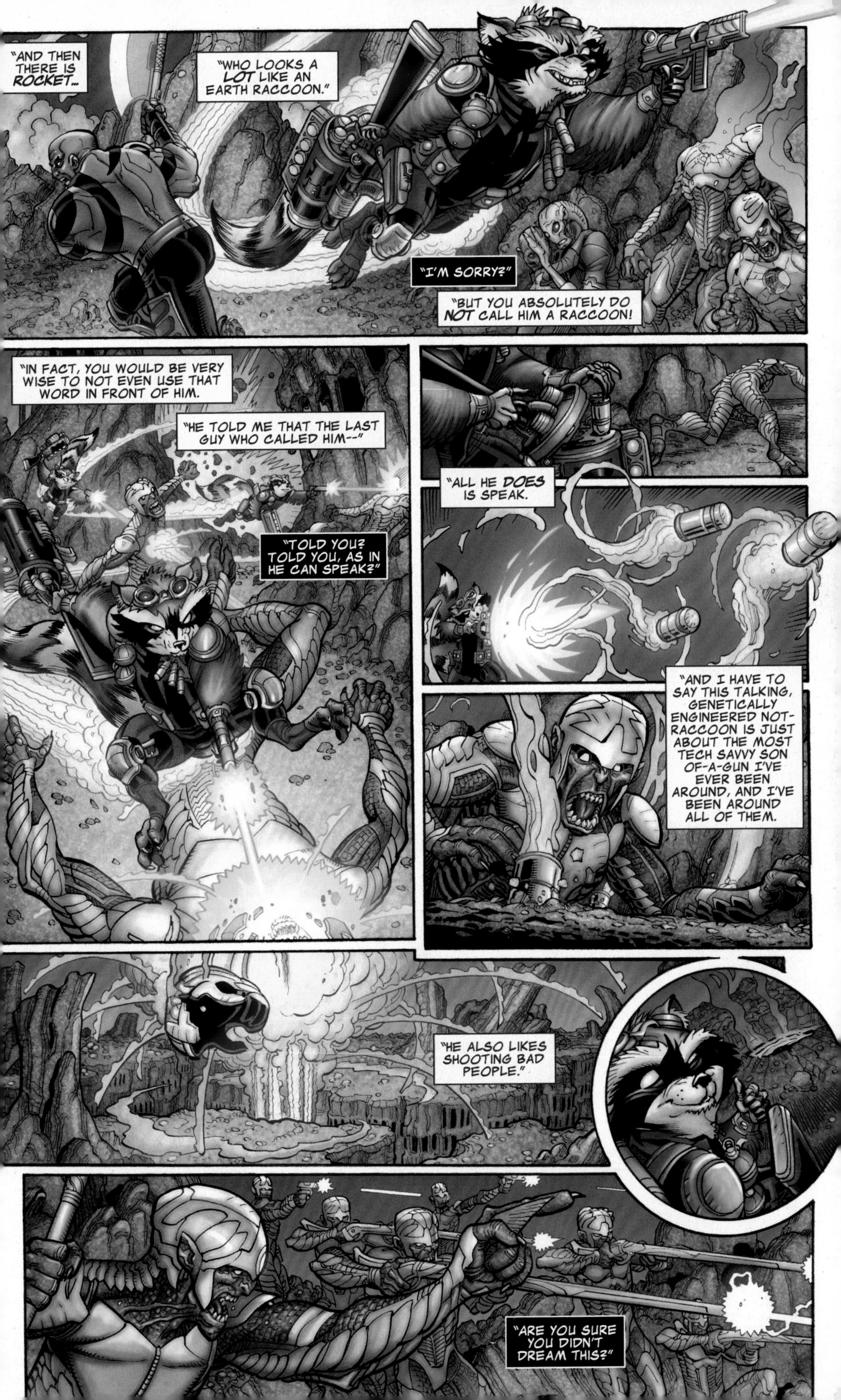

"AND THEN THERE IS ROCKET...
"WHO LOOKS A LOT LIKE AN EARTH RACCOON."
"I'M SORRY?"
"BUT YOU ABSOLUTELY DO NOT CALL HIM A RACCOON!
"IN FACT, YOU WOULD BE VERY WISE TO NOT EVEN USE THAT WORD IN FRONT OF HIM.
"HE TOLD ME THAT THE LAST GUY WHO CALLED HIM--"
"TOLD YOU? TOLD YOU, AS IN HE CAN SPEAK?"
"ALL HE DOES IS SPEAK.
"AND I HAVE TO SAY THIS TALKING, GENETICALLY ENGINEERED NOT-RACCOON IS JUST ABOUT THE MOST TECH SAVVY SON OF-A-GUN I'VE EVER BEEN AROUND, AND I'VE BEEN AROUND ALL OF THEM.
"HE ALSO LIKES SHOOTING BAD PEOPLE."
"ARE YOU SURE YOU DIDN'T DREAM THIS?"

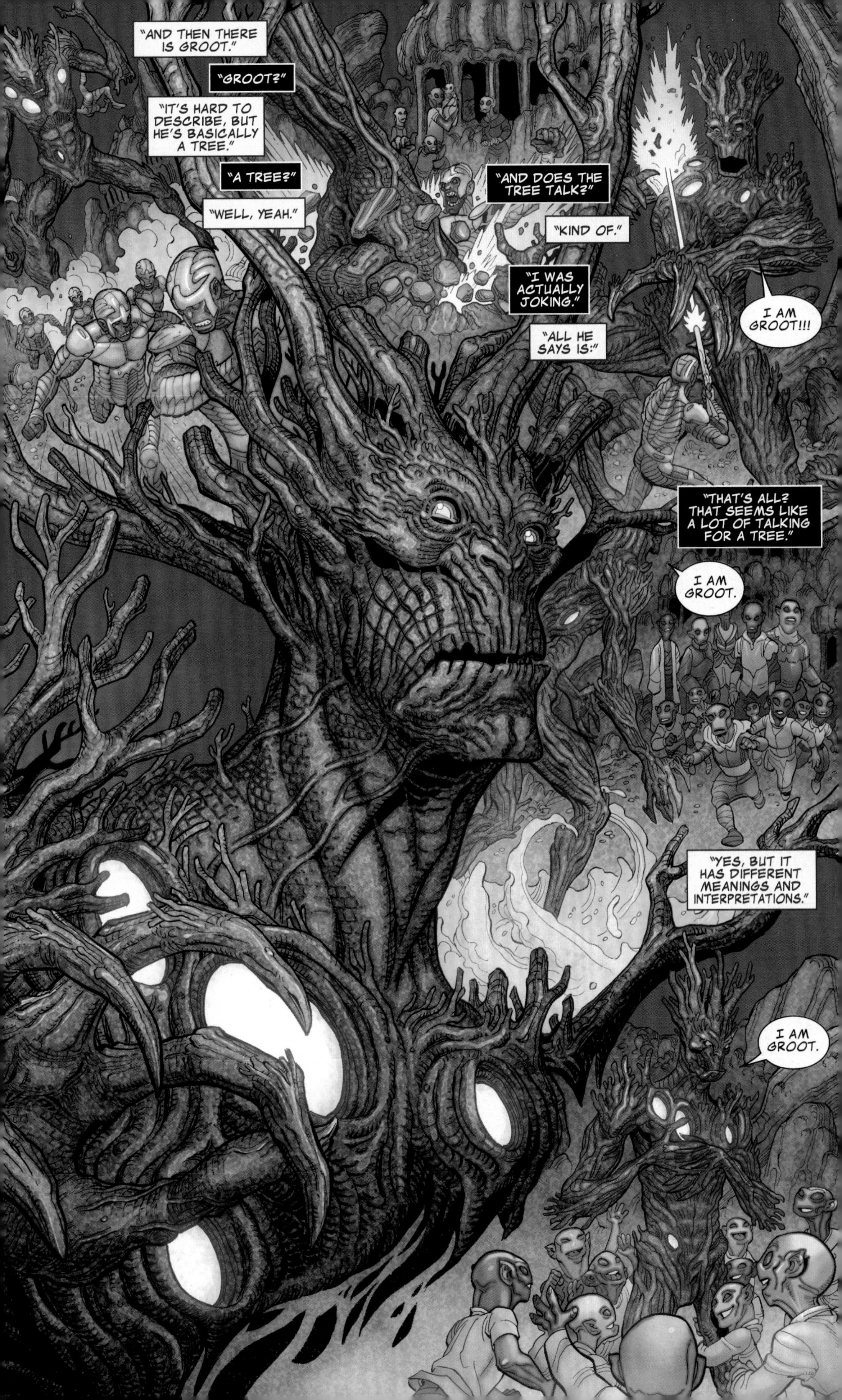
"AND THEN THERE IS GROOT."
"GROOT?"
"IT'S HARD TO DESCRIBE, BUT HE'S BASICALLY A TREE."
"A TREE?"
"WELL, YEAH."
"AND DOES THE TREE TALK?"
"KIND OF."
"I WAS ACTUALLY JOKING."
"ALL HE SAYS IS:"
I AM GROOT!!!
"THAT'S ALL? THAT SEEMS LIKE A LOT OF TALKING FOR A TREE."
I AM GROOT.
"YES, BUT IT HAS DIFFERENT MEANINGS AND INTERPRETATIONS."
I AM GROOT.

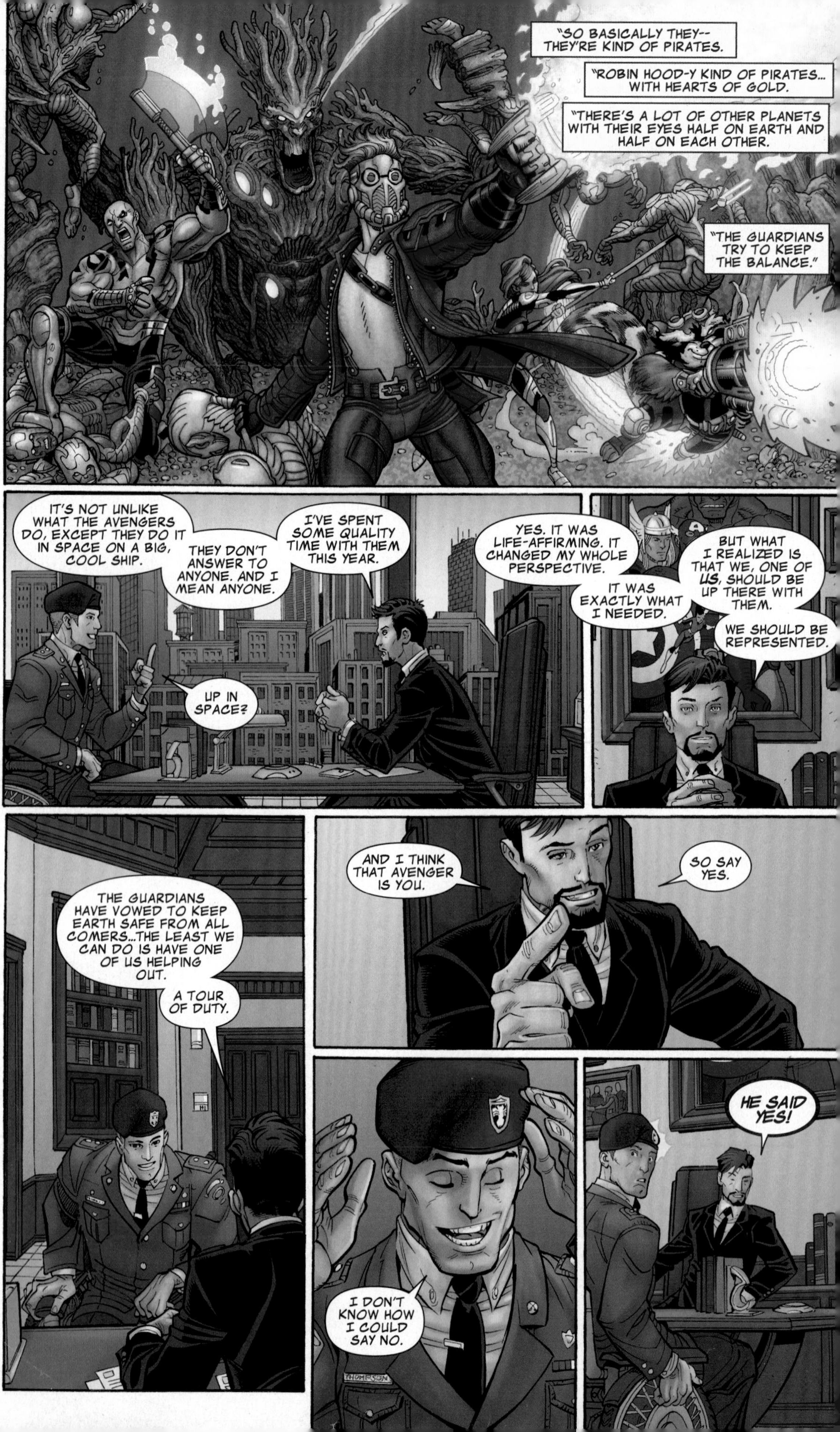
"SO BASICALLY THEY-- THEY'RE KIND OF PIRATES.
"ROBIN HOOD-Y KIND OF PIRATES... WITH HEARTS OF GOLD.
"THERE'S A LOT OF OTHER PLANETS WITH THEIR EYES HALF ON EARTH AND HALF ON EACH OTHER.
"THE GUARDIANS TRY TO KEEP THE BALANCE."
IT'S NOT UNLIKE WHAT THE AVENGERS DO, EXCEPT THEY DO IT IN SPACE ON A BIG, COOL SHIP.
THEY DON'T ANSWER TO ANYONE. AND I MEAN ANYONE.
I'VE SPENT SOME QUALITY TIME WITH THEM THIS YEAR.
UP IN SPACE?
YES. IT WAS LIFE-AFFIRMING. IT CHANGED MY WHOLE PERSPECTIVE.
IT WAS EXACTLY WHAT I NEEDED.
BUT WHAT I REALIZED IS THAT WE, ONE OF US, SHOULD BE UP THERE WITH THEM.
WE SHOULD BE REPRESENTED.
THE GUARDIANS HAVE VOWED TO KEEP EARTH SAFE FROM ALL COMERS...THE LEAST WE CAN DO IS HAVE ONE OF US HELPING OUT.
A TOUR OF DUTY.
AND I THINK THAT AVENGER IS YOU.
SO SAY YES.
I DON'T KNOW HOW I COULD SAY NO.
HE SAID YES!

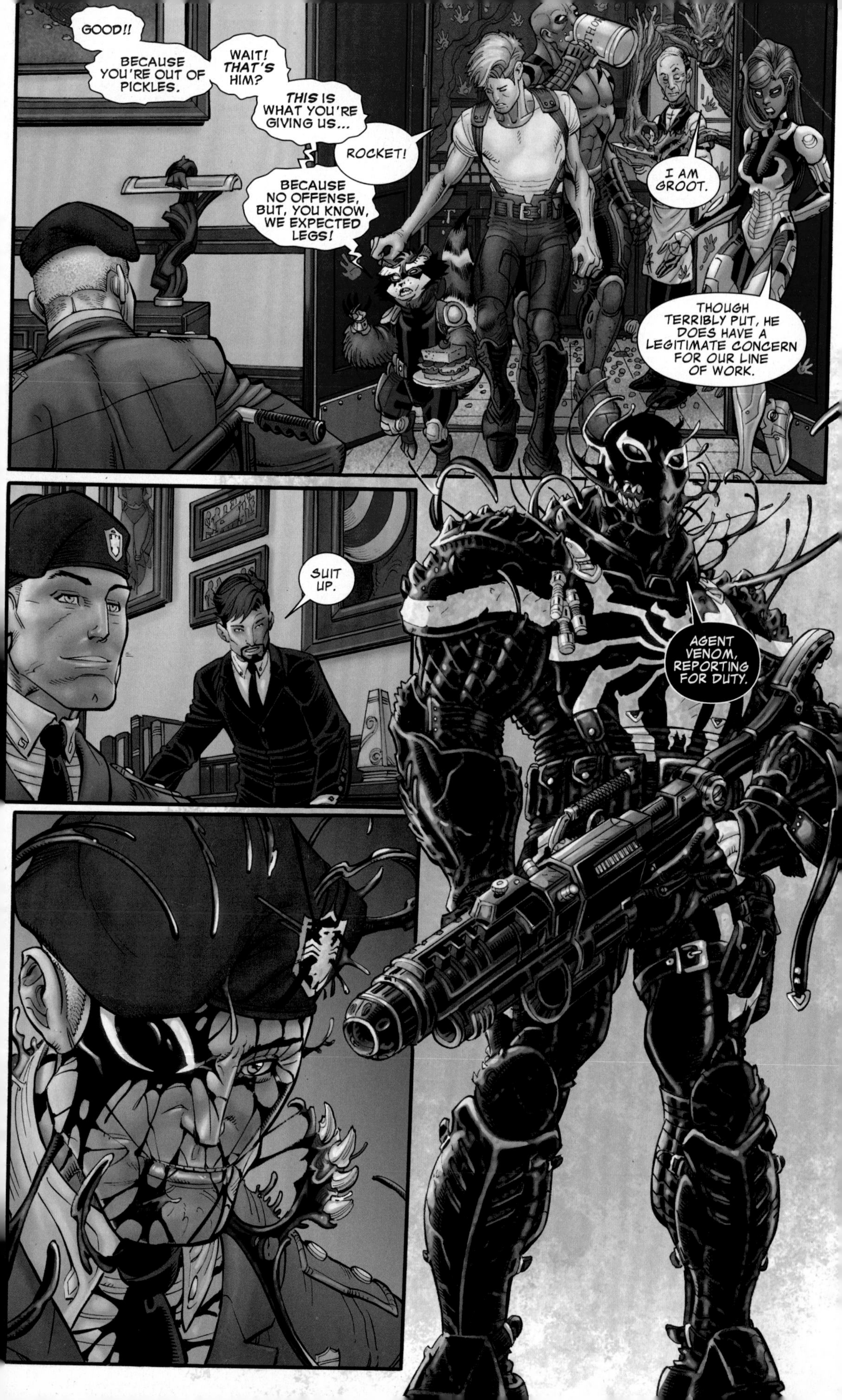
GOOD!!
BECAUSE YOU'RE OUT OF PICKLES.
WAIT! THAT'S HIM?
THIS IS WHAT YOU'RE GIVING US...
ROCKET!
BECAUSE NO OFFENSE, BUT, YOU KNOW, WE EXPECTED LEGS!
I AM GROOT.
THOUGH TERRIBLY PUT, HE DOES HAVE A LEGITIMATE CONCERN FOR OUR LINE OF WORK.
SUIT UP.
AGENT VENOM, REPORTING FOR DUTY.

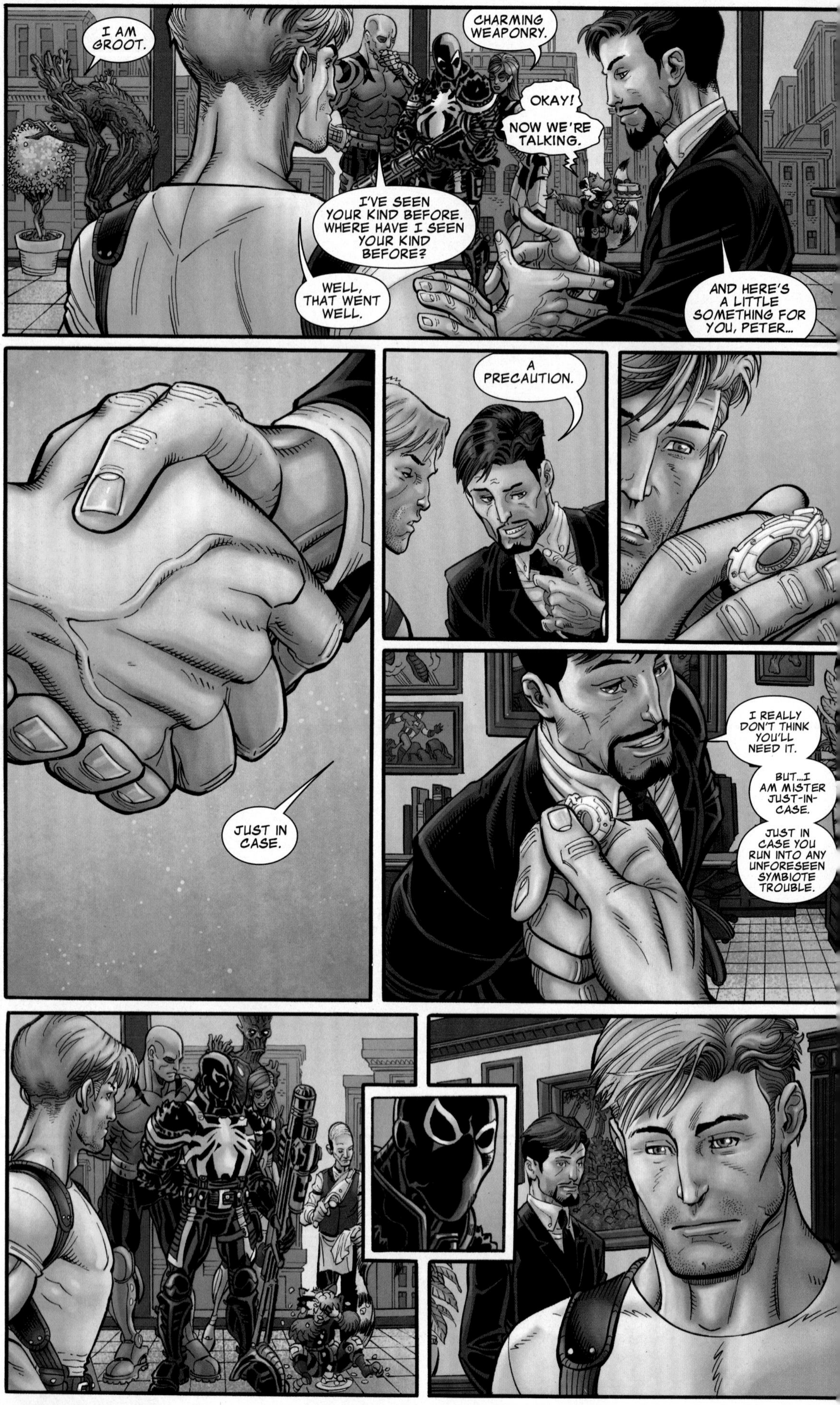
I AM GROOT.
CHARMING WEAPONRY.
OKAY!
NOW WE'RE TALKING.
I'VE SEEN YOUR KIND BEFORE. WHERE HAVE I SEEN YOUR KIND BEFORE?
WELL, THAT WENT WELL.
AND HERE'S A LITTLE SOMETHING FOR YOU, PETER...
A PRECAUTION.
JUST IN CASE.
I REALLY DON'T THINK YOU'LL NEED IT.
BUT...I AM MISTER JUST-IN-CASE.
JUST IN CASE YOU RUN INTO ANY UNFORESEEN SYMBIOTE TROUBLE.

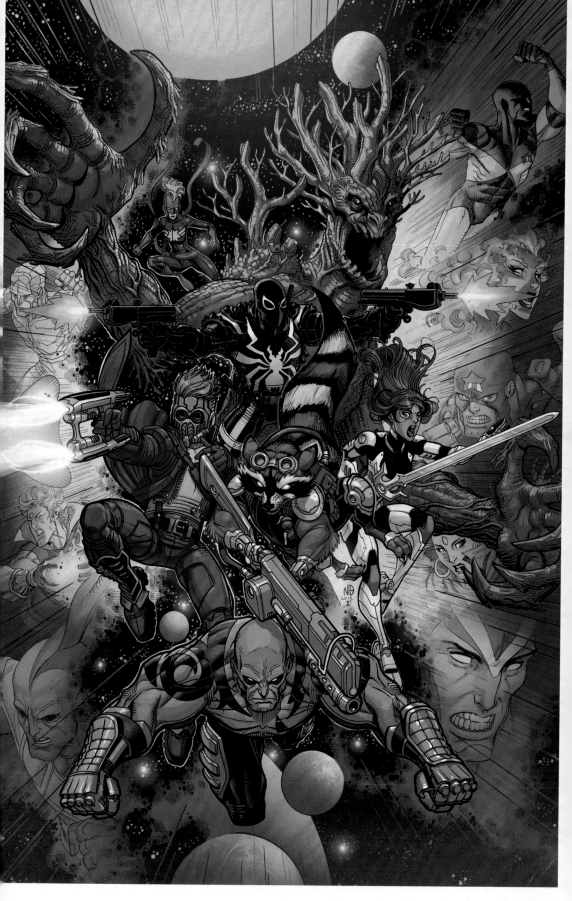

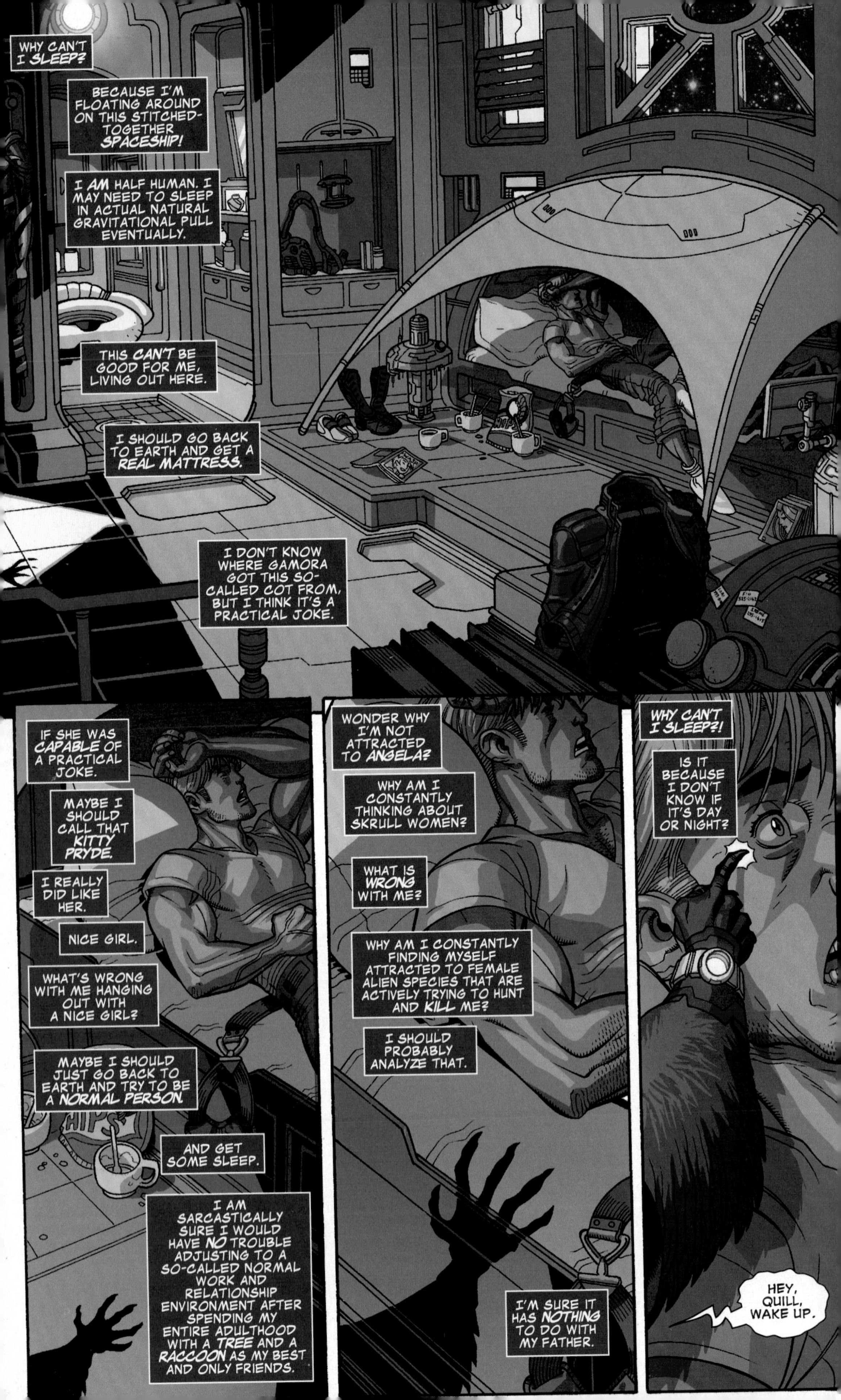

WHY CAN'T I SLEEP?
BECAUSE I'M FLOATING AROUND ON THIS STITCHED-TOGETHER SPACESHIP!
I AM HALF HUMAN. I MAY NEED TO SLEEP IN ACTUAL NATURAL GRAVITATIONAL PULL EVENTUALLY.
THIS CAN'T BE GOOD FOR ME, LIVING OUT HERE.
I SHOULD GO BACK TO EARTH AND GET A REAL MATTRESS.
I DON'T KNOW WHERE GAMORA GOT THIS SO-CALLED COT FROM, BUT I THINK IT'S A PRACTICAL JOKE.
IF SHE WAS CAPABLE OF A PRACTICAL JOKE.
MAYBE I SHOULD CALL THAT KITTY PRYDE.
I REALLY DID LIKE HER.
NICE GIRL.
WHAT'S WRONG WITH ME HANGING OUT WITH A NICE GIRL?
MAYBE I SHOULD JUST GO BACK TO EARTH AND TRY TO BE A NORMAL PERSON.
AND GET SOME SLEEP.
I AM SARCASTICALLY SURE I WOULD HAVE NO TROUBLE ADJUSTING TO A SO-CALLED NORMAL WORK AND RELATIONSHIP ENVIRONMENT AFTER SPENDING MY ENTIRE ADULTHOOD WITH A TREE AND A RACCOON AS MY BEST AND ONLY FRIENDS.
WONDER WHY I'M NOT ATTRACTED TO ANGELA?
WHY AM I CONSTANTLY THINKING ABOUT SKRULL WOMEN?
WHAT IS WRONG WITH ME?
WHY AM I CONSTANTLY FINDING MYSELF ATTRACTED TO FEMALE ALIEN SPECIES THAT ARE ACTIVELY TRYING TO HUNT AND KILL ME?
I SHOULD PROBABLY ANALYZE THAT.
I'M SURE IT HAS NOTHING TO DO WITH MY FATHER.
WHY CAN'T I SLEEP?!
IS IT BECAUSE I DON'T KNOW IF IT'S DAY OR NIGHT?
HEY, QUILL, WAKE UP.

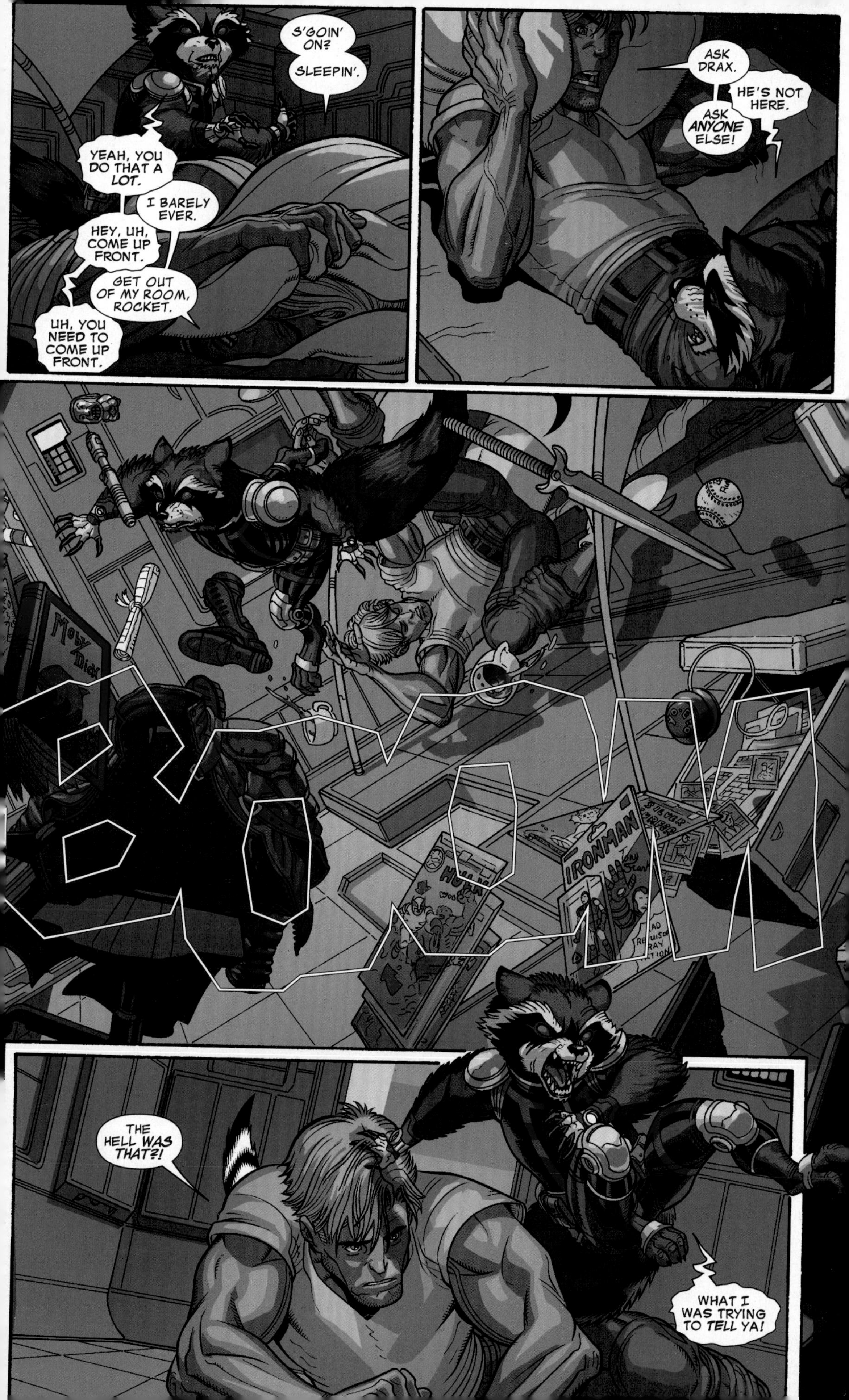
S'GOIN' ON?
SLEEPIN'.
YEAH, YOU DO THAT A LOT.
I BARELY EVER.
HEY, UH, COME UP FRONT.
GET OUT OF MY ROOM, ROCKET.
UH, YOU NEED TO COME UP FRONT.
ASK DRAX.
HE'S NOT HERE.
ASK ANYONE ELSE!
BOOM
THE HELL WAS THAT?!
WHAT I WAS TRYING TO TELL YA!

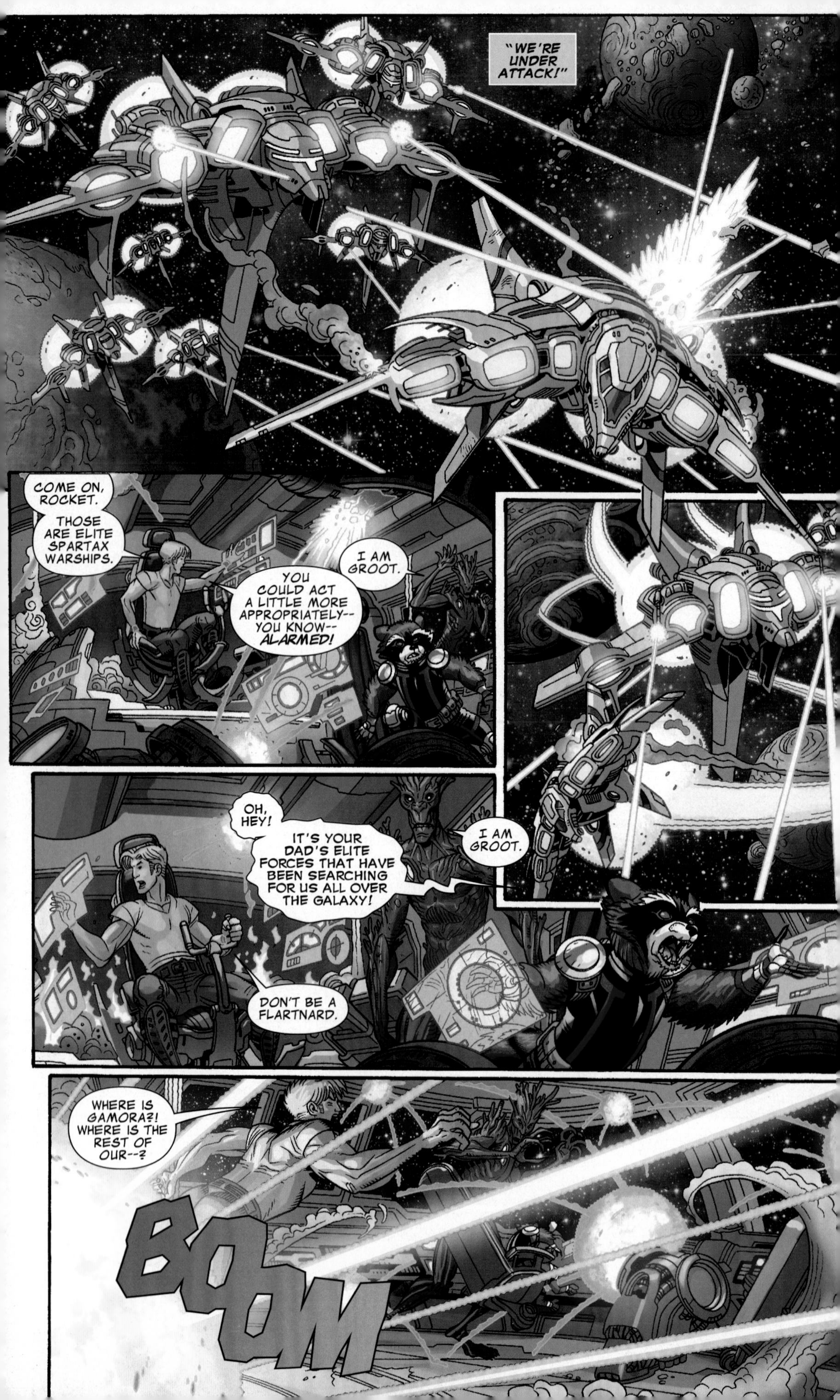
"WE'RE UNDER ATTACK!"
COME ON, ROCKET.
THOSE ARE ELITE SPARTAX WARSHIPS.
YOU COULD ACT A LITTLE MORE APPROPRIATELY-- YOU KNOW-- ALARMED!
I AM GROOT.
OH, HEY!
IT'S YOUR DAD'S ELITE FORCES THAT HAVE BEEN SEARCHING FOR US ALL OVER THE GALAXY!
I AM GROOT.
DON'T BE A FLARTNARD.
WHERE IS GAMORA?! WHERE IS THE REST OF OUR--?
BOOM

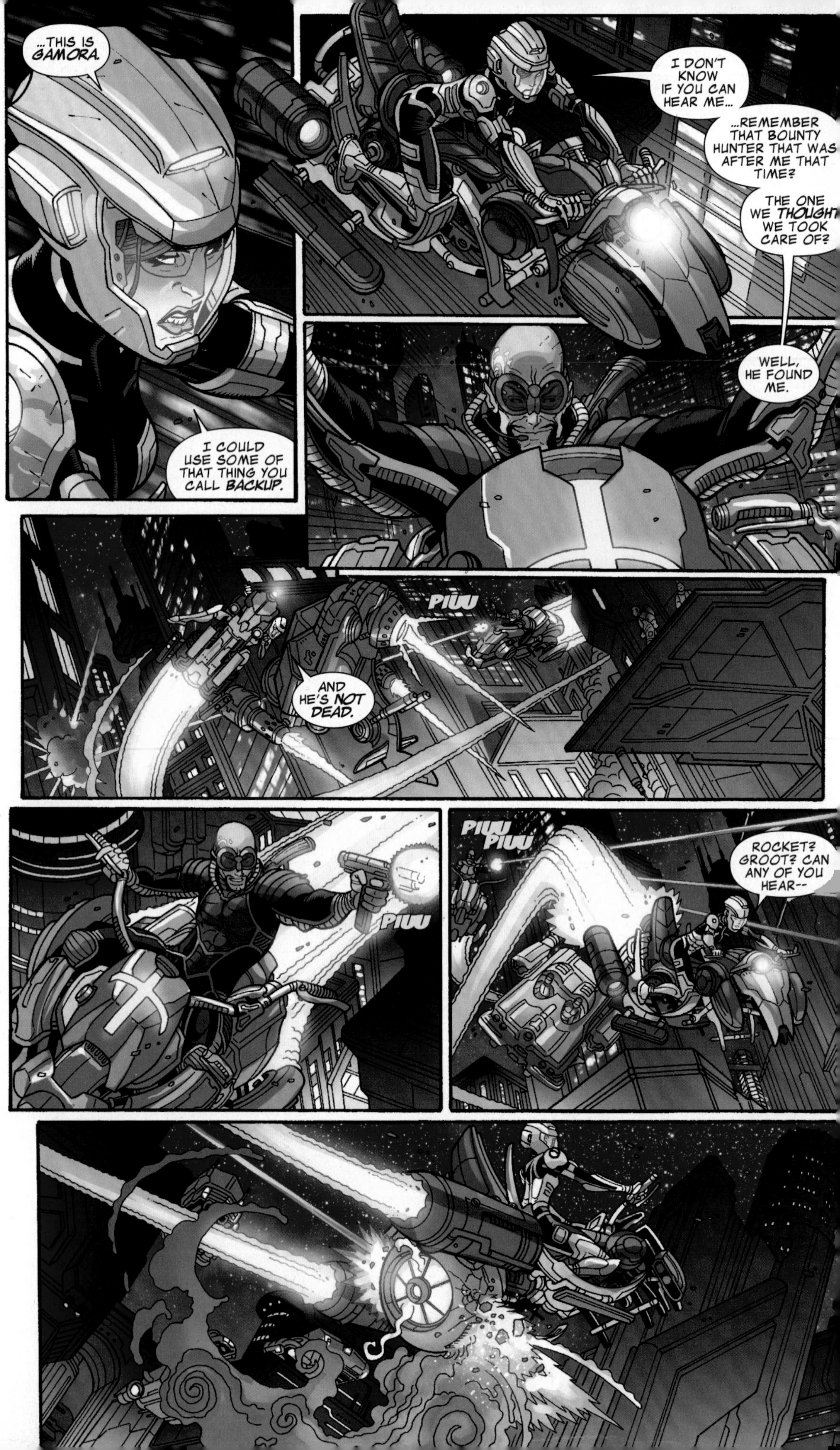
...THIS IS GAMORA.
I COULD USE SOME OF THAT THING YOU CALL BACKUP.
I DON'T KNOW IF YOU CAN HEAR ME...
...REMEMBER THAT BOUNTY HUNTER THAT WAS AFTER ME THAT TIME?
THE ONE WE THOUGHT WE TOOK CARE OF?
WELL, HE FOUND ME.
PIUU
AND HE'S NOT DEAD.
PIUU
PIUU PIUU
ROCKET? GROOT? CAN ANY OF YOU HEAR--

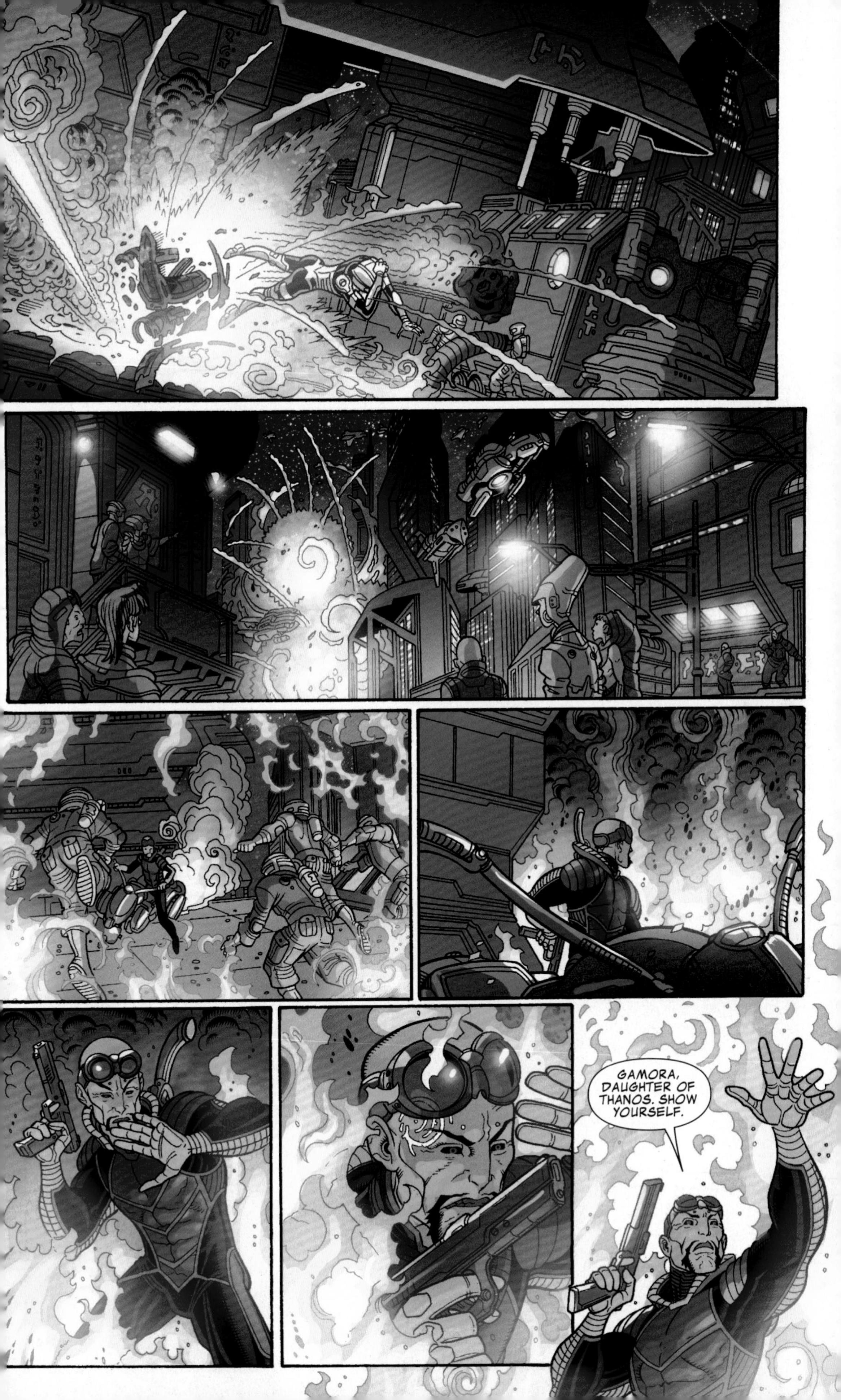
GAMORA, DAUGHTER OF THANOS. SHOW YOURSELF.

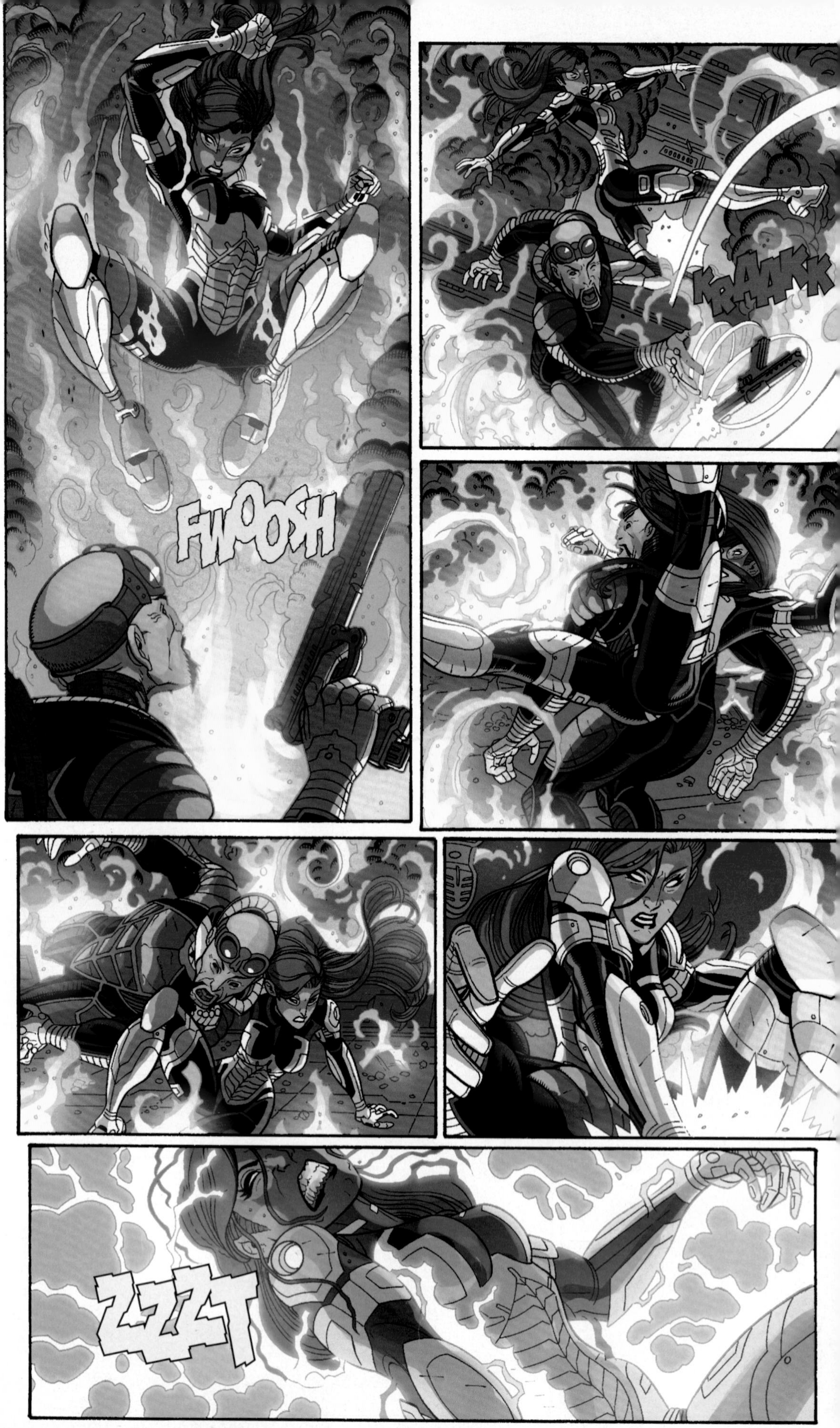
FWOOSH
KRAAKK
ZZZT

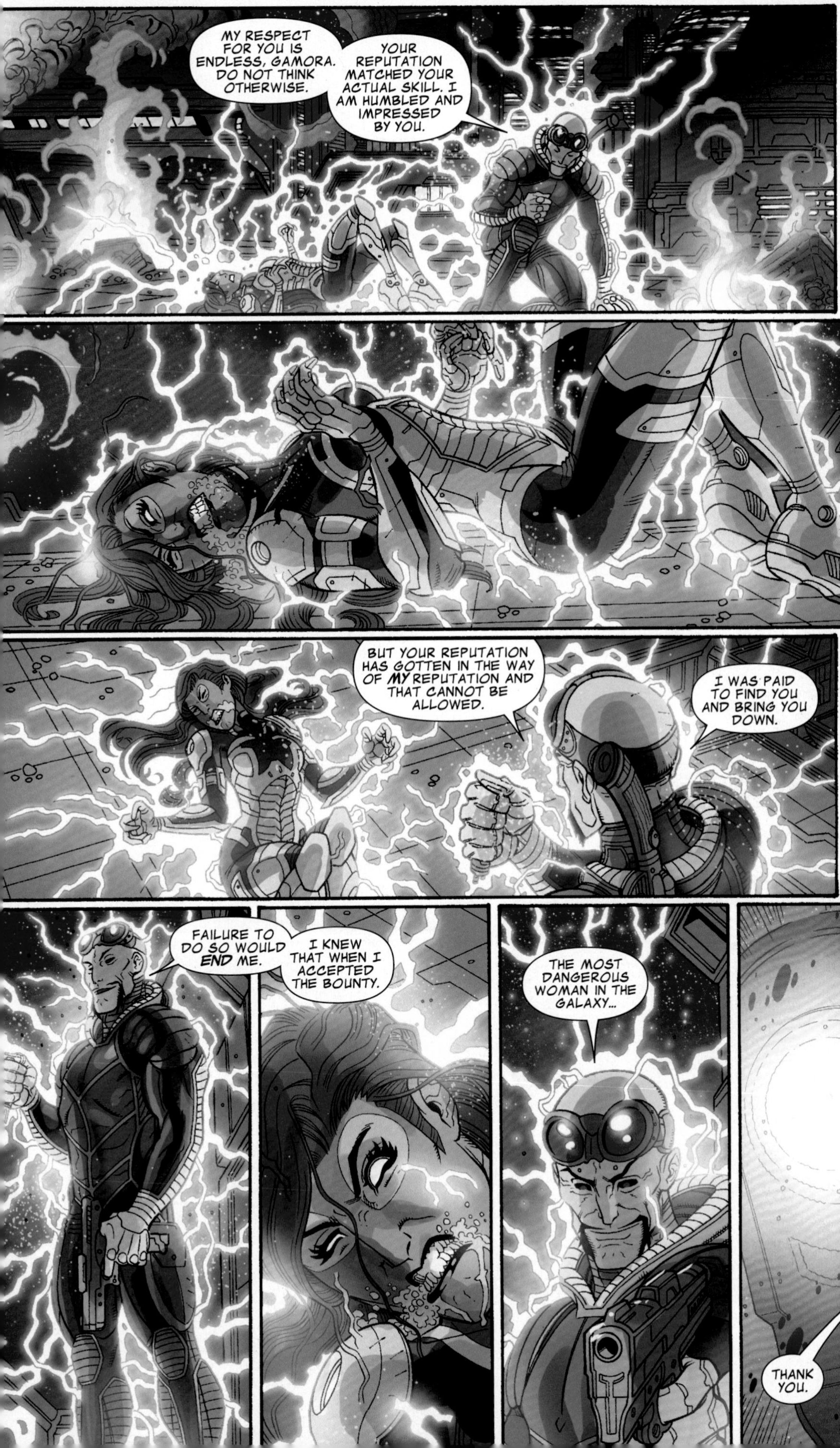
MY RESPECT FOR YOU IS ENDLESS, GAMORA. DO NOT THINK OTHERWISE.
YOUR REPUTATION MATCHED YOUR ACTUAL SKILL. I AM HUMBLED AND IMPRESSED BY YOU.
BUT YOUR REPUTATION HAS GOTTEN IN THE WAY OF MY REPUTATION AND THAT CANNOT BE ALLOWED.
I WAS PAID TO FIND YOU AND BRING YOU DOWN.
FAILURE TO DO SO WOULD END ME.
I KNEW THAT WHEN I ACCEPTED THE BOUNTY.
THE MOST DANGEROUS WOMAN IN THE GALAXY...
THANK YOU.

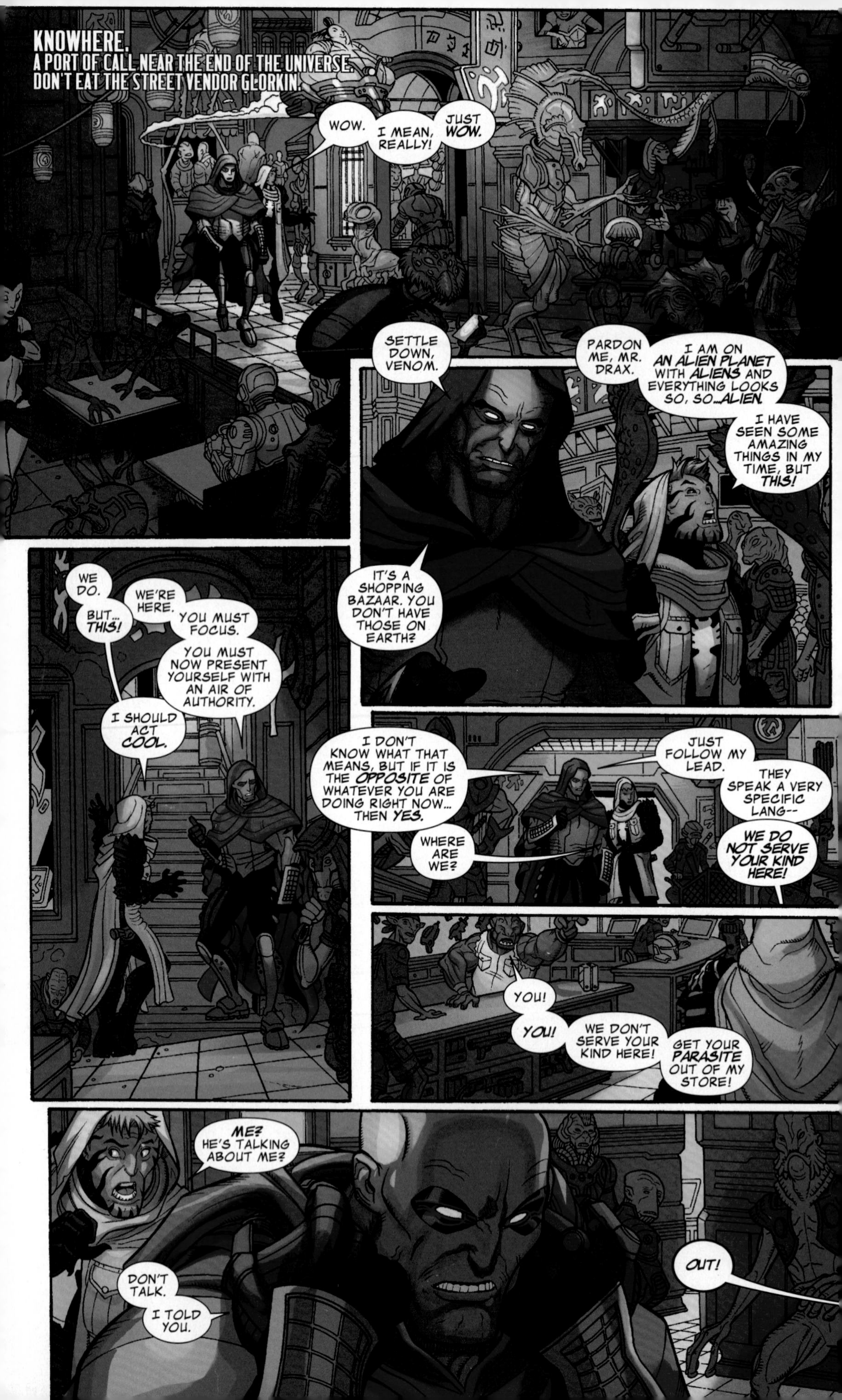
KNOWHERE.
A PORT OF CALL NEAR THE END OF THE UNIVERSE.
DON'T EAT THE STREET VENDOR GLORKIN.
WOW.
I MEAN, REALLY!
JUST WOW.
SETTLE DOWN, VENOM.
PARDON ME, MR. DRAX.
I AM ON AN ALIEN PLANET WITH ALIENS AND EVERYTHING LOOKS SO, SO...ALIEN.
I HAVE SEEN SOME AMAZING THINGS IN MY TIME, BUT THIS!
IT'S A SHOPPING BAZAAR. YOU DON'T HAVE THOSE ON EARTH?
WE DO.
BUT... THIS!
WE'RE HERE.
YOU MUST FOCUS.
YOU MUST NOW PRESENT YOURSELF WITH AN AIR OF AUTHORITY.
I SHOULD ACT COOL.
I DON'T KNOW WHAT THAT MEANS, BUT IF IT IS THE OPPOSITE OF WHATEVER YOU ARE DOING RIGHT NOW... THEN YES.
WHERE ARE WE?
JUST FOLLOW MY LEAD.
THEY SPEAK A VERY SPECIFIC LANG--
WE DO NOT SERVE YOUR KIND HERE!
YOU!
YOU!
WE DON'T SERVE YOUR KIND HERE!
GET YOUR PARASITE OUT OF MY STORE!
ME? HE'S TALKING ABOUT ME?
DON'T TALK.
I TOLD YOU.
OUT!

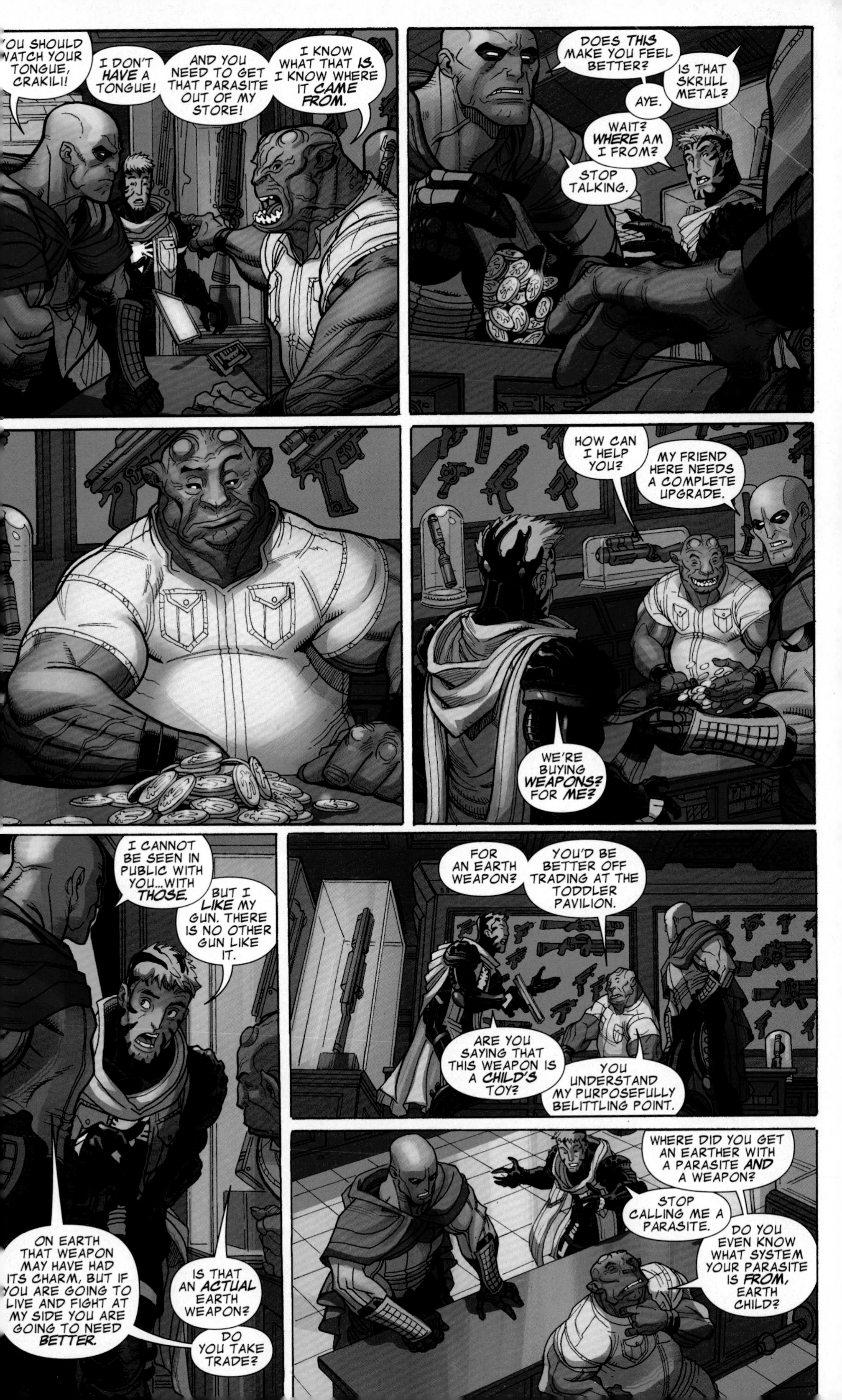

YOU SHOULD WATCH YOUR TONGUE, CRAKILI!
I DON'T HAVE A TONGUE!
AND YOU NEED TO GET THAT PARASITE OUT OF MY STORE!
I KNOW WHAT THAT IS. I KNOW WHERE IT CAME FROM.
DOES THIS MAKE YOU FEEL BETTER?
IS THAT SKRULL METAL?
AYE.
WAIT? WHERE AM I FROM?
STOP TALKING.
HOW CAN I HELP YOU?
MY FRIEND HERE NEEDS A COMPLETE UPGRADE.
WE'RE BUYING WEAPONS? FOR ME?
I CANNOT BE SEEN IN PUBLIC WITH YOU...WITH THOSE.
BUT I LIKE MY GUN. THERE IS NO OTHER GUN LIKE IT.
ON EARTH THAT WEAPON MAY HAVE HAD ITS CHARM, BUT IF YOU ARE GOING TO LIVE AND FIGHT AT MY SIDE YOU ARE GOING TO NEED BETTER.
IS THAT AN ACTUAL EARTH WEAPON?
DO YOU TAKE TRADE?
FOR AN EARTH WEAPON?
YOU'D BE BETTER OFF TRADING AT THE TODDLER PAVILION.
ARE YOU SAYING THAT THIS WEAPON IS A CHILD'S TOY?
YOU UNDERSTAND MY PURPOSEFULLY BELITTLING POINT.
WHERE DID YOU GET AN EARTHER WITH A PARASITE AND A WEAPON?
STOP CALLING ME A PARASITE.
DO YOU EVEN KNOW WHAT SYSTEM YOUR PARASITE IS FROM, EARTH CHILD?

UM...

...THE SYMBIOTE PLANET?

NOW I SEE WHY YOU KEEP HIM AROUND.

HE'S FUNNY.

LET'S SEE.

WE DON'T WANT TO GIVE HIM ANYTHING *TOO* DANGEROUS.

WE *WANT* DANGEROUS.

RIGHT?

UM...

...YES?

OFF THIS PLANET.

I STILL CAN'T *BELIEVE* I'M NOT ON THE ONE I *LIVE* ON.

WHAT DID THAT, WHATEVER THAT WAS BACK THERE, MEAN ABOUT ME AND MY--?

HE IS A *CRAKILI* AND HE IS A FOOL.

I'M--HEY, I'M *ASKING* YOU.

DO YOU ALL KNOW SOMETHING ABOUT MY SYMBIOTE THAT I *DON'T KNOW?*

I'M ASKING BECAUSE I LEFT EVERYTH[ING] IN MY LIFE BEH[IND] ON EARTH T[O] COME OUT HE[RE] AND HELP YOU GUARDIANS O[F] THE GALAXY.

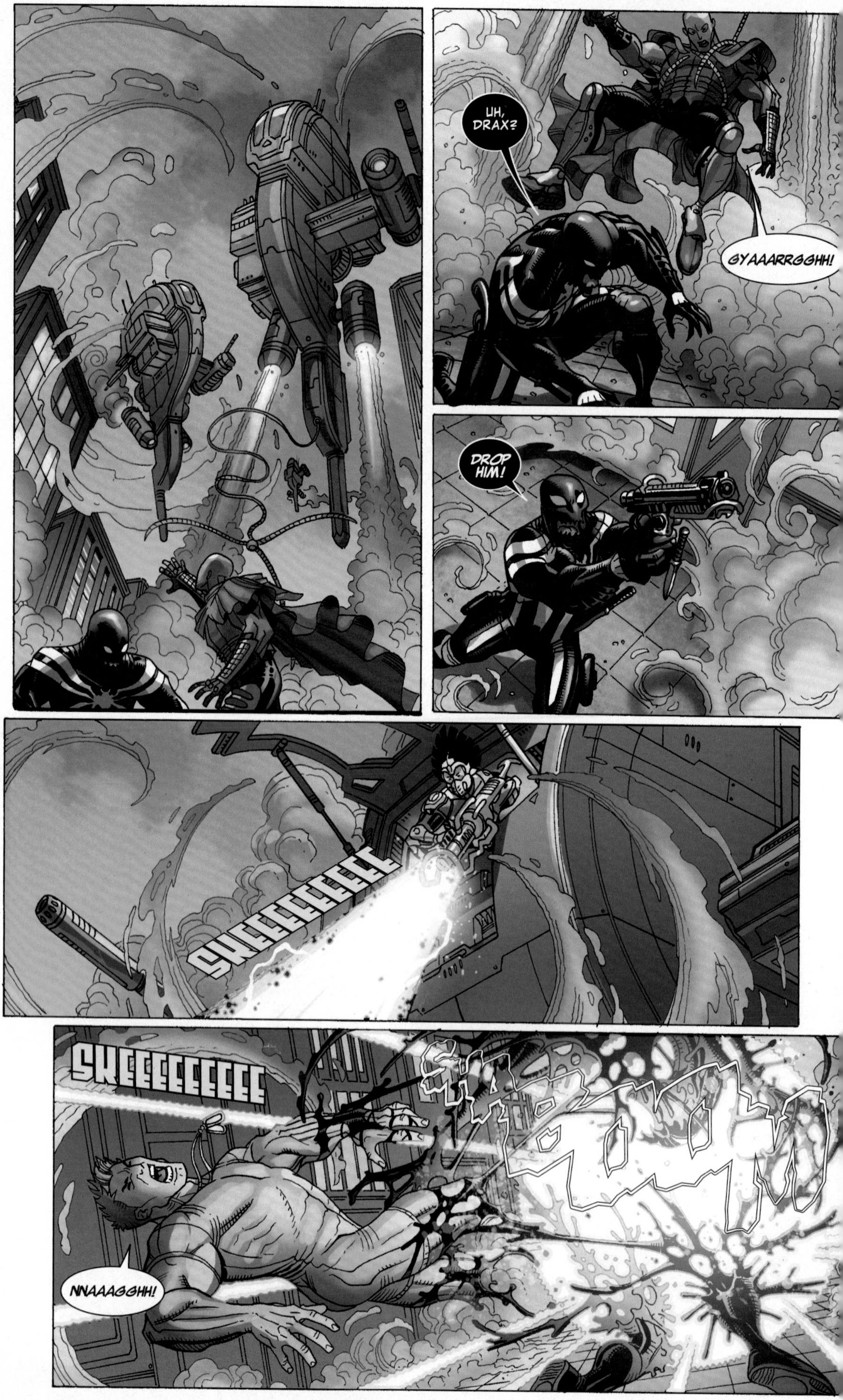
UH, DRAX?
GYAAARRGGHH!
DROP HIM!
SKEEEEEEEE
SKEEEEEEEEE
NNAAAGGHH!

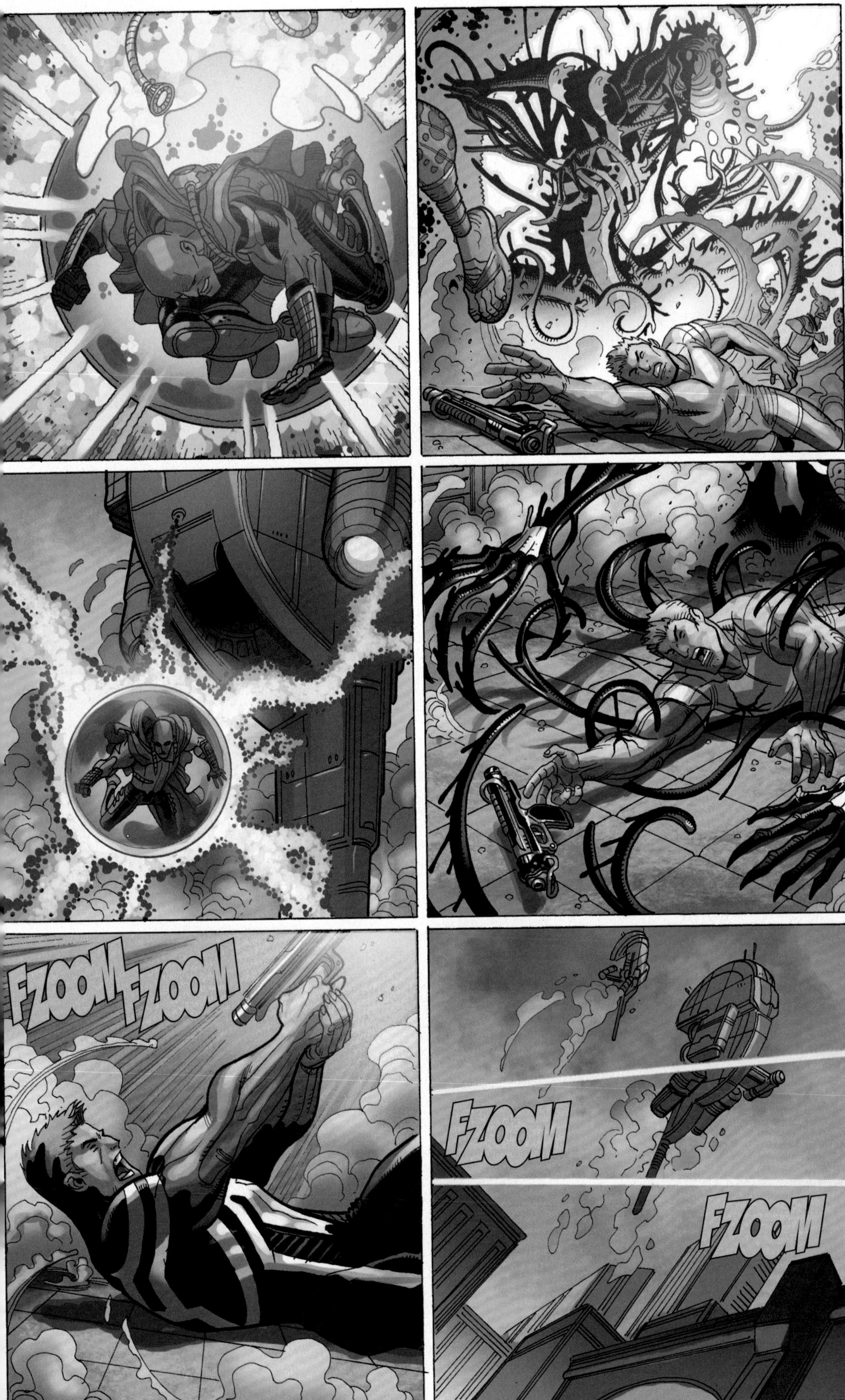
FZOOM FZOOM
FZOOM
FZOOM

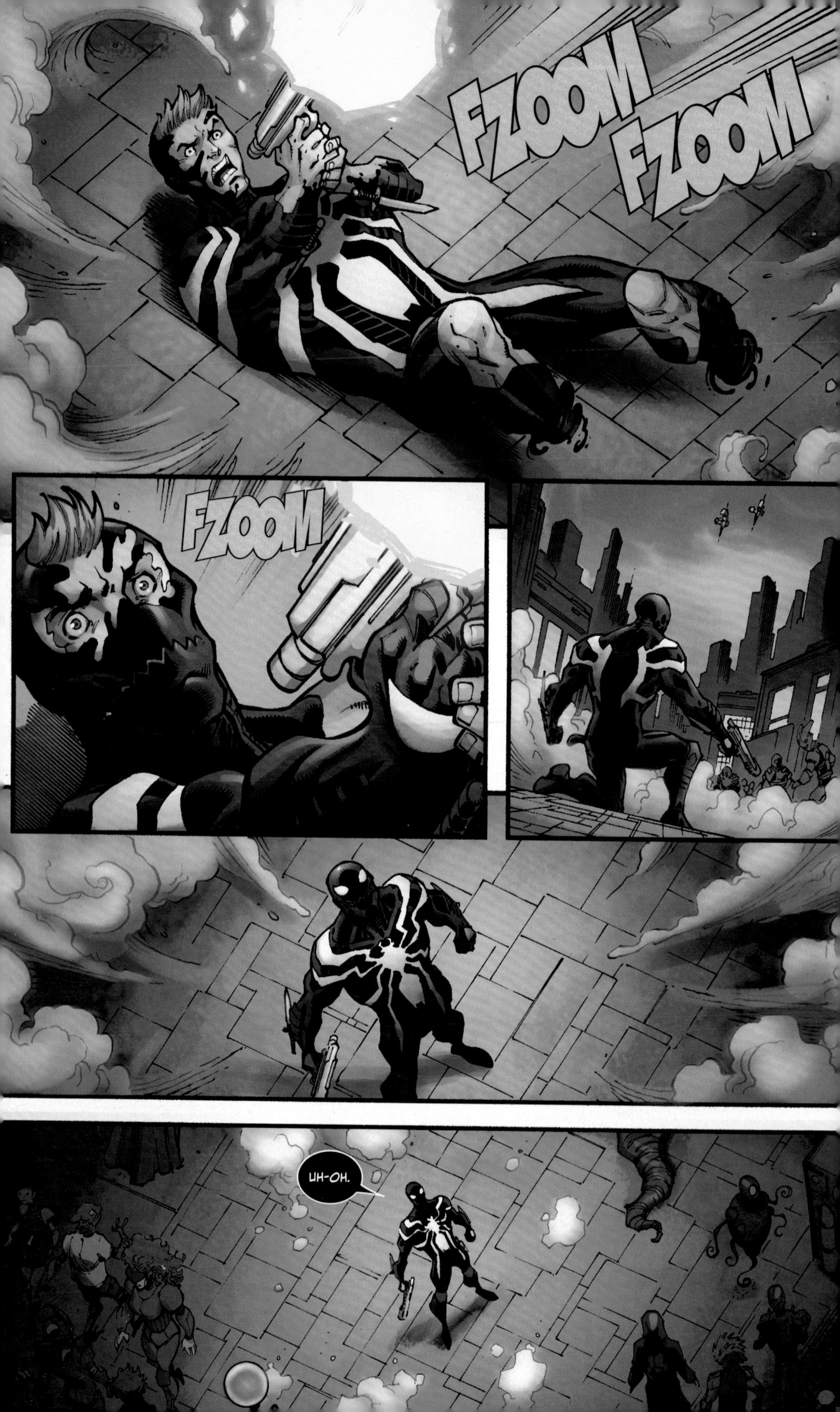
FZOOM
FZOOM
FZOOM
UH-OH.

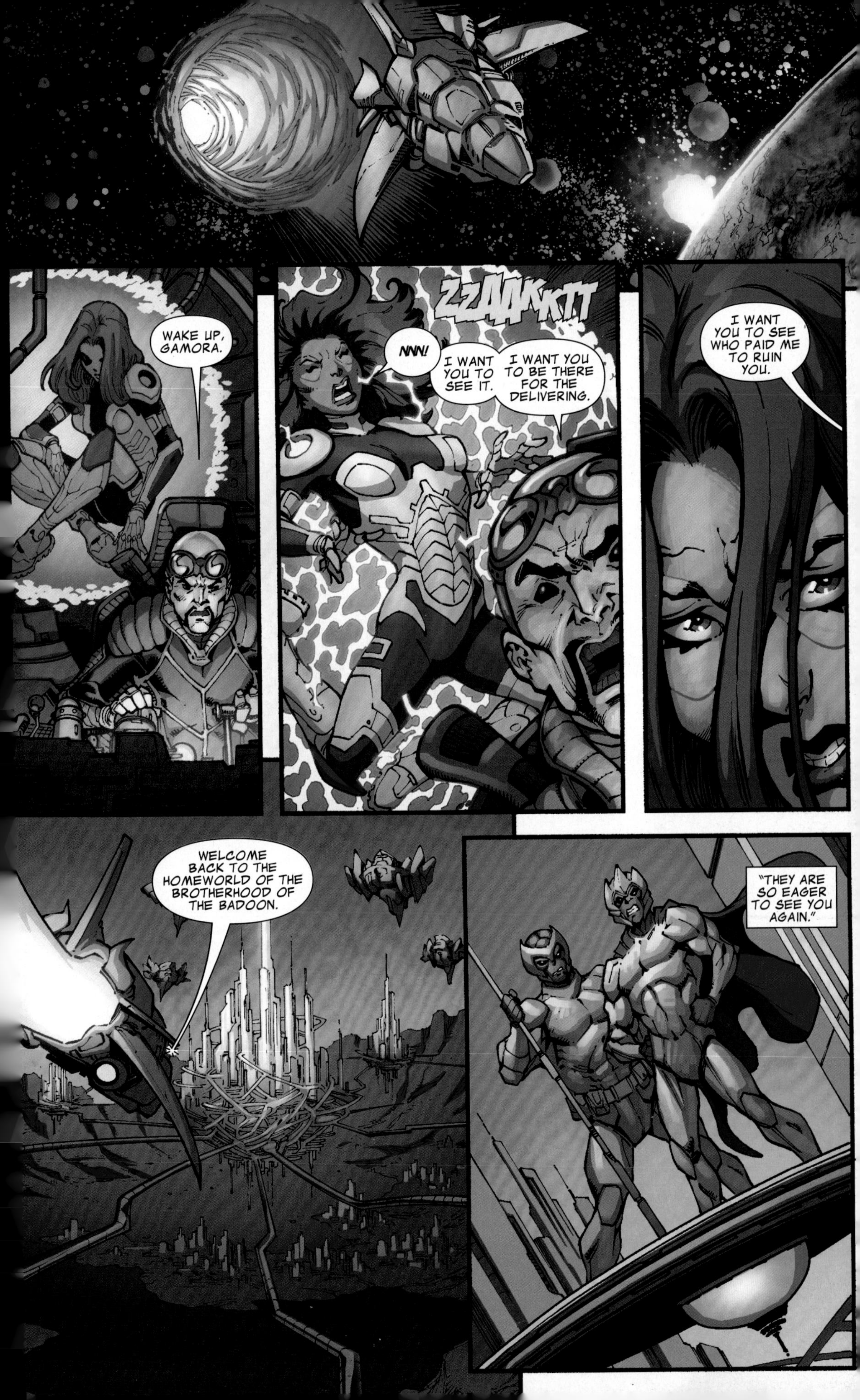
WAKE UP, GAMORA.
ZZAAKKTT
NNN!
I WANT YOU TO SEE IT.
I WANT YOU TO BE THERE FOR THE DELIVERING.
I WANT YOU TO SEE WHO PAID ME TO RUIN YOU.
WELCOME BACK TO THE HOMEWORLD OF THE BROTHERHOOD OF THE BADOON.
"THEY ARE SO EAGER TO SEE YOU AGAIN."

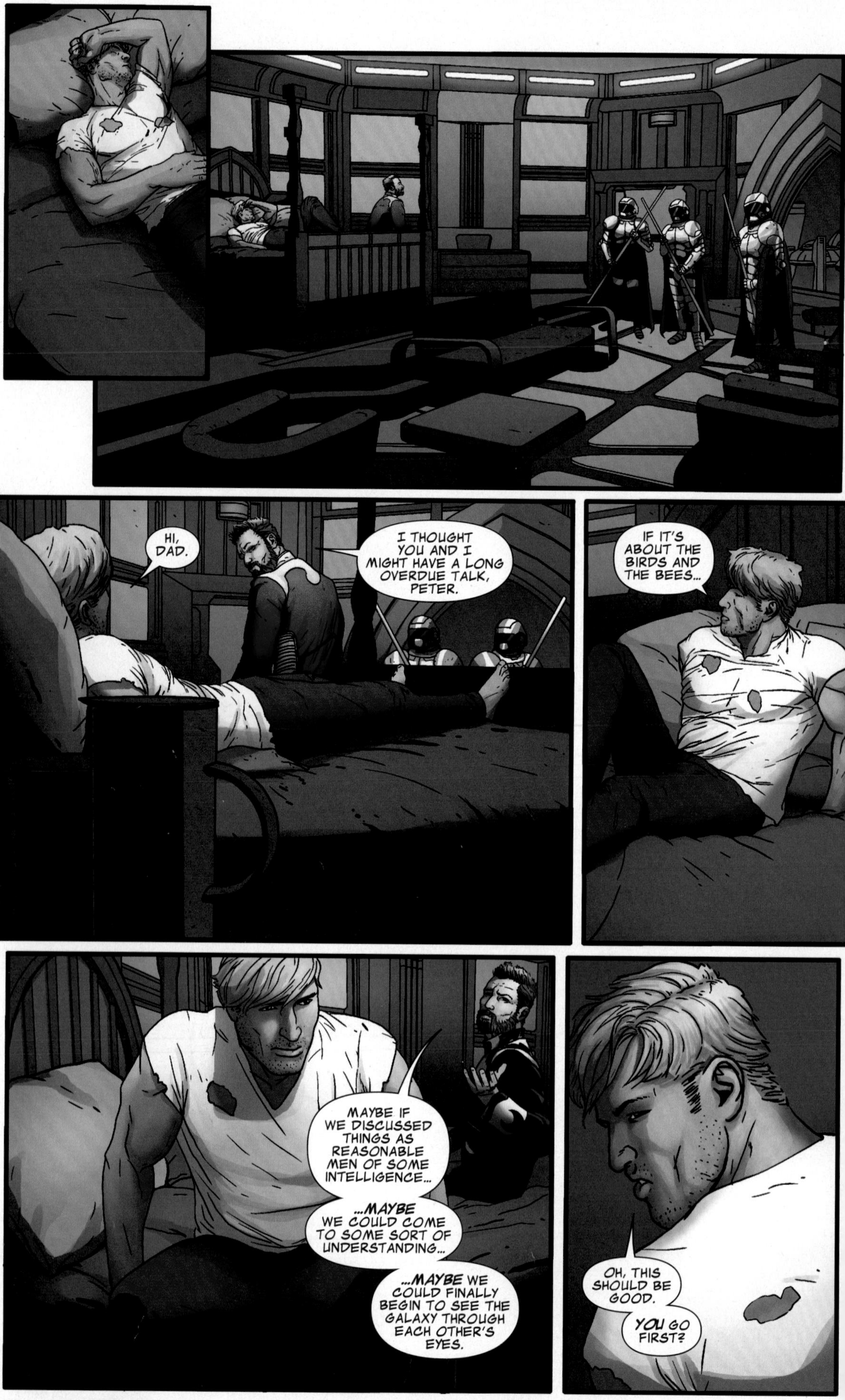
HI, DAD.
I THOUGHT YOU AND I MIGHT HAVE A LONG OVERDUE TALK, PETER.
IF IT'S ABOUT THE BIRDS AND THE BEES...
MAYBE IF WE DISCUSSED THINGS AS REASONABLE MEN OF SOME INTELLIGENCE...
...MAYBE WE COULD COME TO SOME SORT OF UNDERSTANDING...
...MAYBE WE COULD FINALLY BEGIN TO SEE THE GALAXY THROUGH EACH OTHER'S EYES.
OH, THIS SHOULD BE GOOD.
YOU GO FIRST?

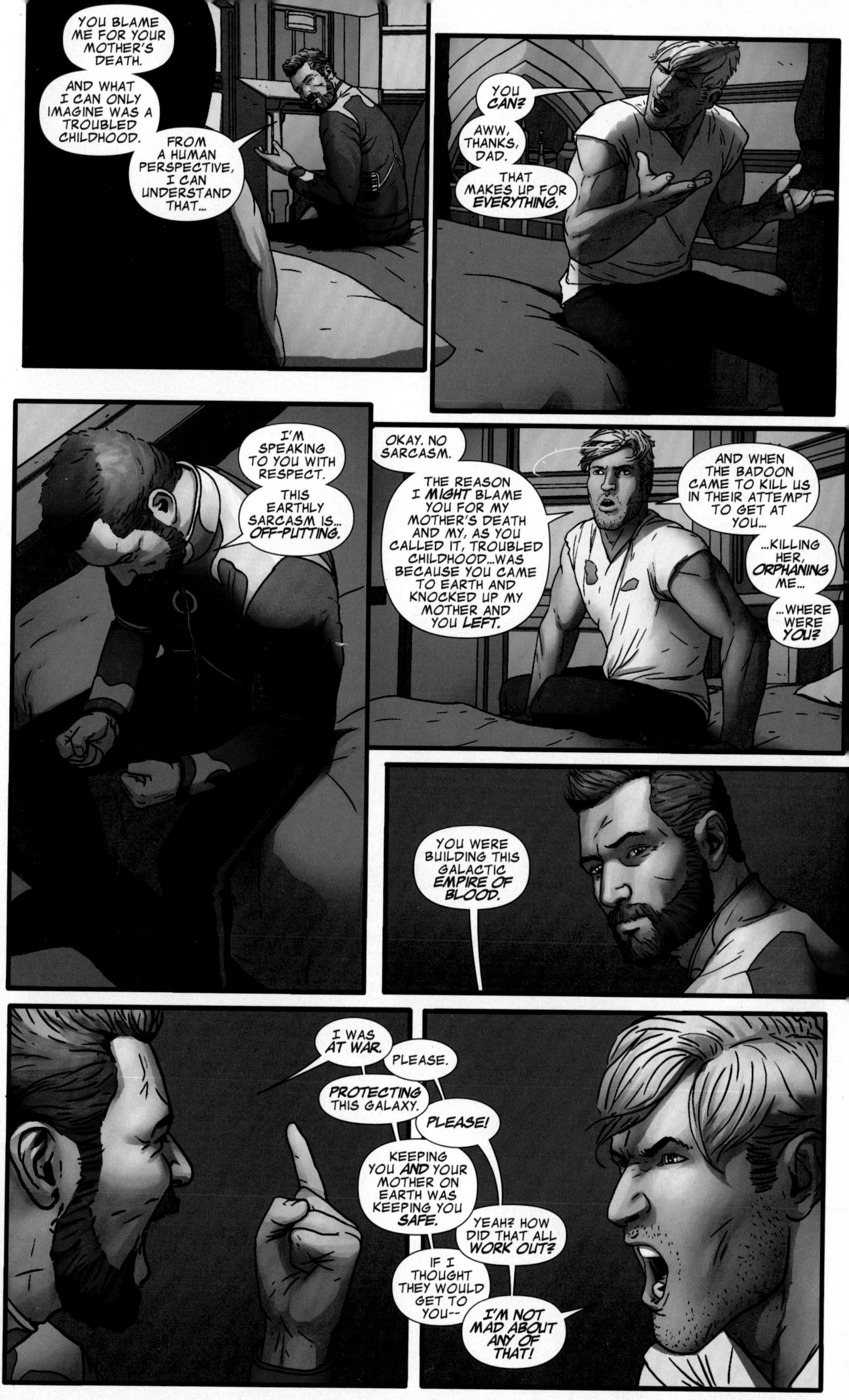

YOU BLAME ME FOR YOUR MOTHER'S DEATH.
AND WHAT I CAN ONLY IMAGINE WAS A TROUBLED CHILDHOOD.
FROM A HUMAN PERSPECTIVE, I CAN UNDERSTAND THAT...
YOU CAN?
AWW, THANKS, DAD.
THAT MAKES UP FOR EVERYTHING.
I'M SPEAKING TO YOU WITH RESPECT.
THIS EARTHLY SARCASM IS... OFF-PUTTING.
OKAY. NO SARCASM.
THE REASON I MIGHT BLAME YOU FOR MY MOTHER'S DEATH AND MY, AS YOU CALLED IT, TROUBLED CHILDHOOD...WAS BECAUSE YOU CAME TO EARTH AND KNOCKED UP MY MOTHER AND YOU LEFT.
AND WHEN THE BADOON CAME TO KILL US IN THEIR ATTEMPT TO GET AT YOU...
...KILLING HER, ORPHANING ME...
...WHERE WERE YOU?
YOU WERE BUILDING THIS GALACTIC EMPIRE OF BLOOD.
I WAS AT WAR.
PLEASE.
PROTECTING THIS GALAXY.
PLEASE!
KEEPING YOU AND YOUR MOTHER ON EARTH WAS KEEPING YOU SAFE.
YEAH? HOW DID THAT ALL WORK OUT?
IF I THOUGHT THEY WOULD GET TO YOU--
I'M NOT MAD ABOUT ANY OF THAT!

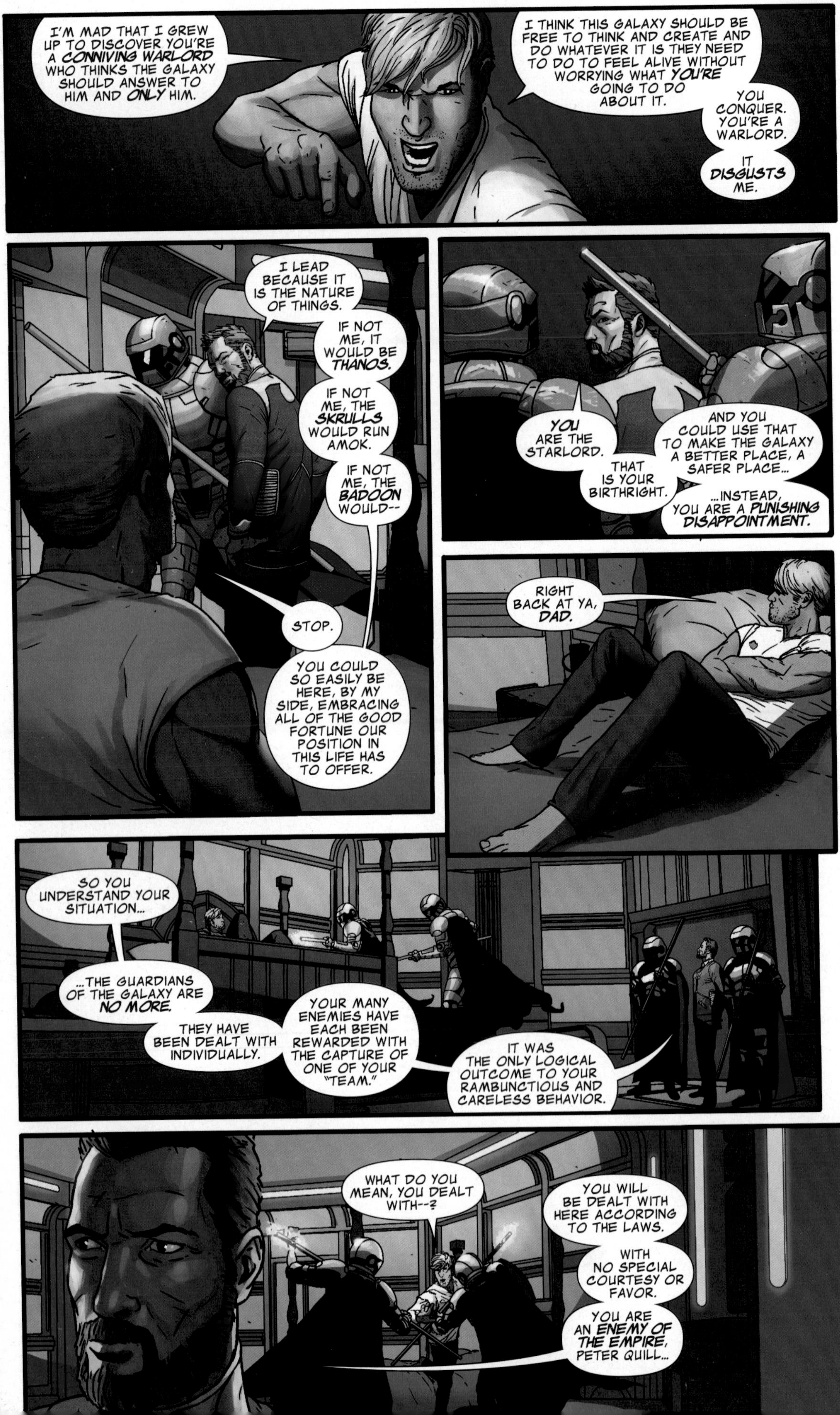
I'M MAD THAT I GREW UP TO DISCOVER YOU'RE A CONNIVING WARLORD WHO THINKS THE GALAXY SHOULD ANSWER TO HIM AND ONLY HIM.
I THINK THIS GALAXY SHOULD BE FREE TO THINK AND CREATE AND DO WHATEVER IT IS THEY NEED TO DO TO FEEL ALIVE WITHOUT WORRYING WHAT YOU'RE GOING TO DO ABOUT IT.
YOU CONQUER. YOU'RE A WARLORD.
IT DISGUSTS ME.
I LEAD BECAUSE IT IS THE NATURE OF THINGS.
IF NOT ME, IT WOULD BE THANOS.
IF NOT ME, THE SKRULLS WOULD RUN AMOK.
IF NOT ME, THE BADOON WOULD--
STOP.
YOU COULD SO EASILY BE HERE, BY MY SIDE, EMBRACING ALL OF THE GOOD FORTUNE OUR POSITION IN THIS LIFE HAS TO OFFER.
YOU ARE THE STARLORD.
THAT IS YOUR BIRTHRIGHT.
AND YOU COULD USE THAT TO MAKE THE GALAXY A BETTER PLACE, A SAFER PLACE...
...INSTEAD, YOU ARE A PUNISHING DISAPPOINTMENT.
RIGHT BACK AT YA, DAD.
SO YOU UNDERSTAND YOUR SITUATION...
...THE GUARDIANS OF THE GALAXY ARE NO MORE.
THEY HAVE BEEN DEALT WITH INDIVIDUALLY.
YOUR MANY ENEMIES HAVE EACH BEEN REWARDED WITH THE CAPTURE OF ONE OF YOUR "TEAM."
IT WAS THE ONLY LOGICAL OUTCOME TO YOUR RAMBUNCTIOUS AND CARELESS BEHAVIOR.
WHAT DO YOU MEAN, YOU DEALT WITH--?
YOU WILL BE DEALT WITH HERE ACCORDING TO THE LAWS.
WITH NO SPECIAL COURTESY OR FAVOR.
YOU ARE AN ENEMY OF THE EMPIRE, PETER QUILL...

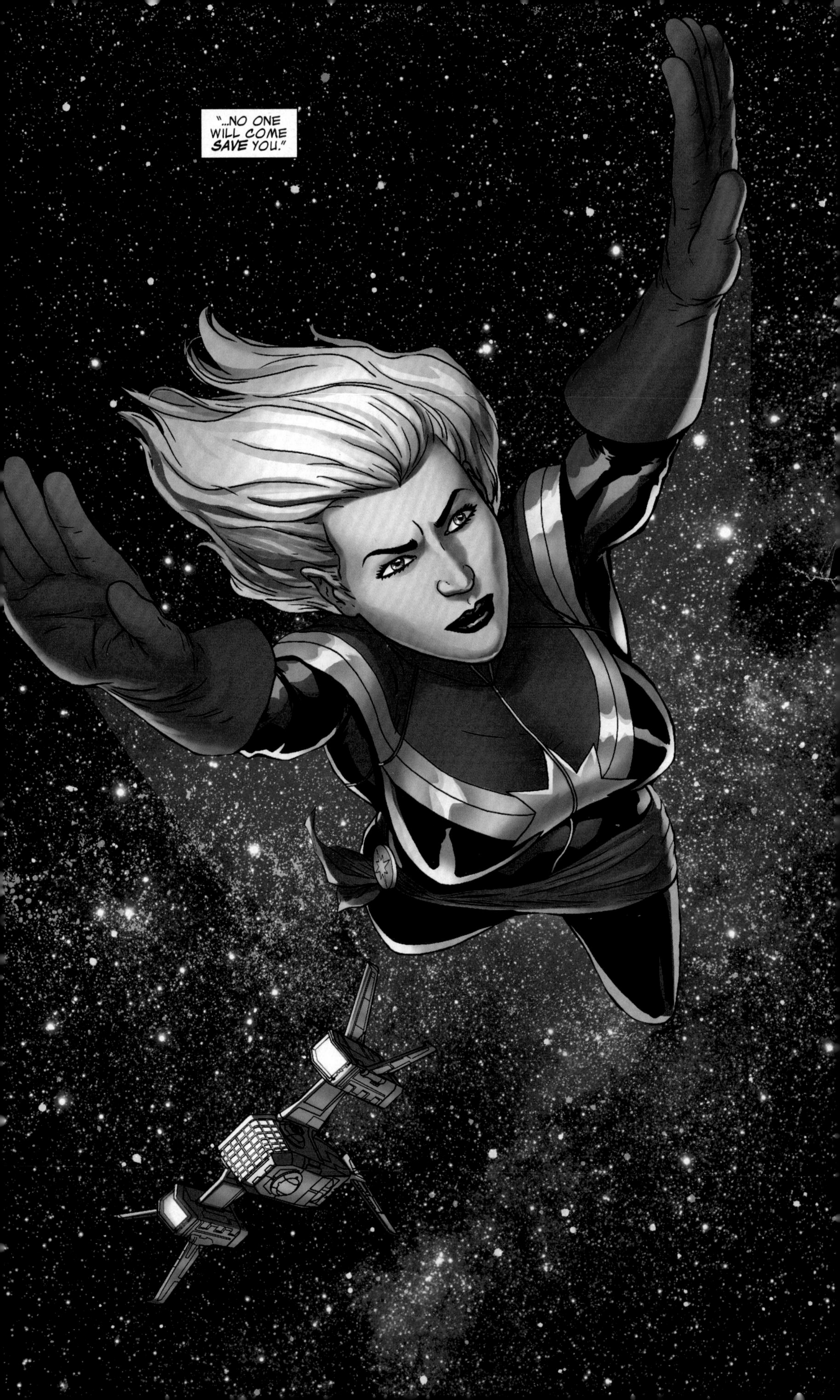
"...NO ONE WILL COME SAVE YOU."

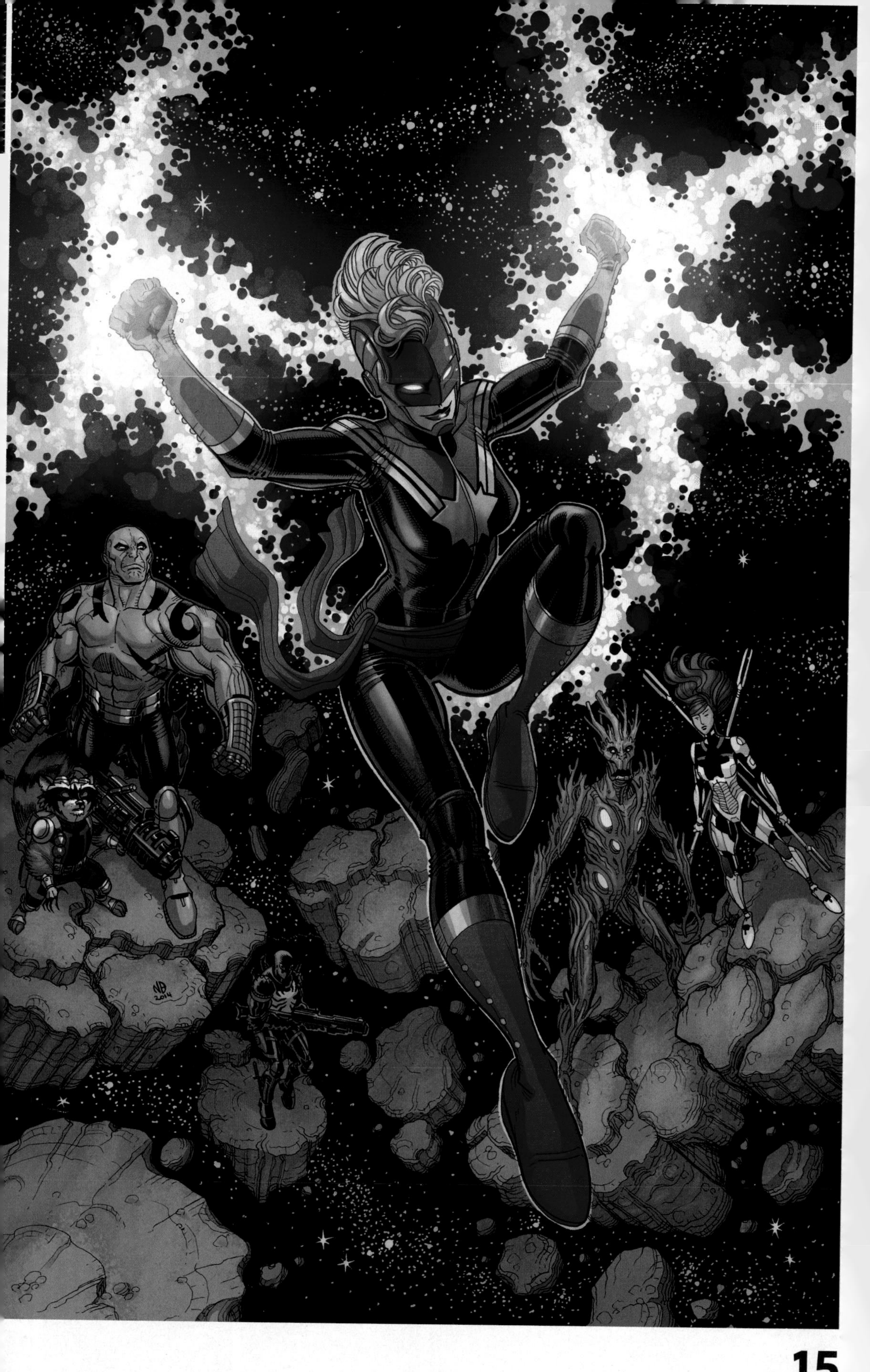

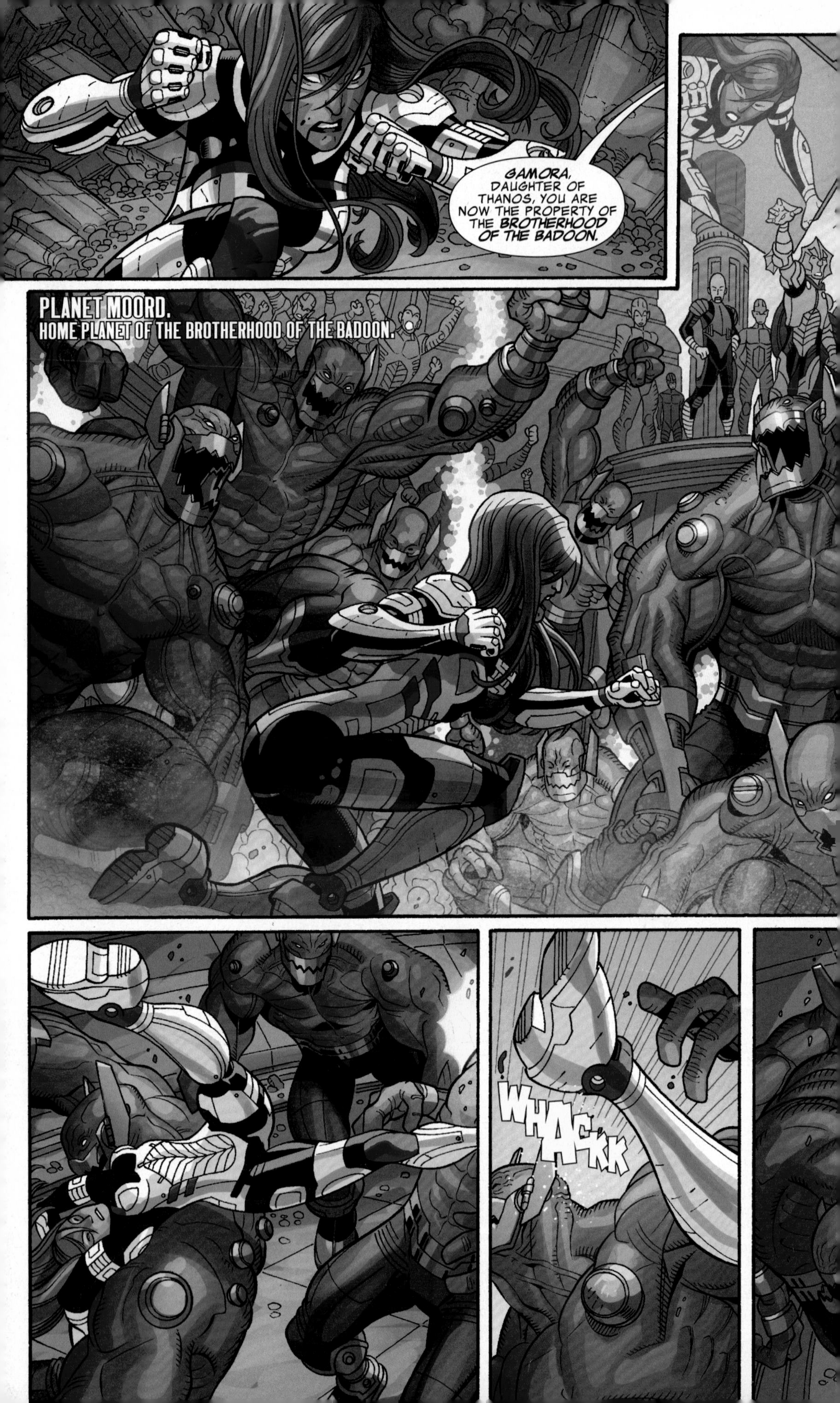
GAMORA, DAUGHTER OF THANOS, YOU ARE NOW THE PROPERTY OF THE BROTHERHOOD OF THE BADOON.
PLANET MOORD.
HOME PLANET OF THE BROTHERHOOD OF THE BADOON.
WHACKK

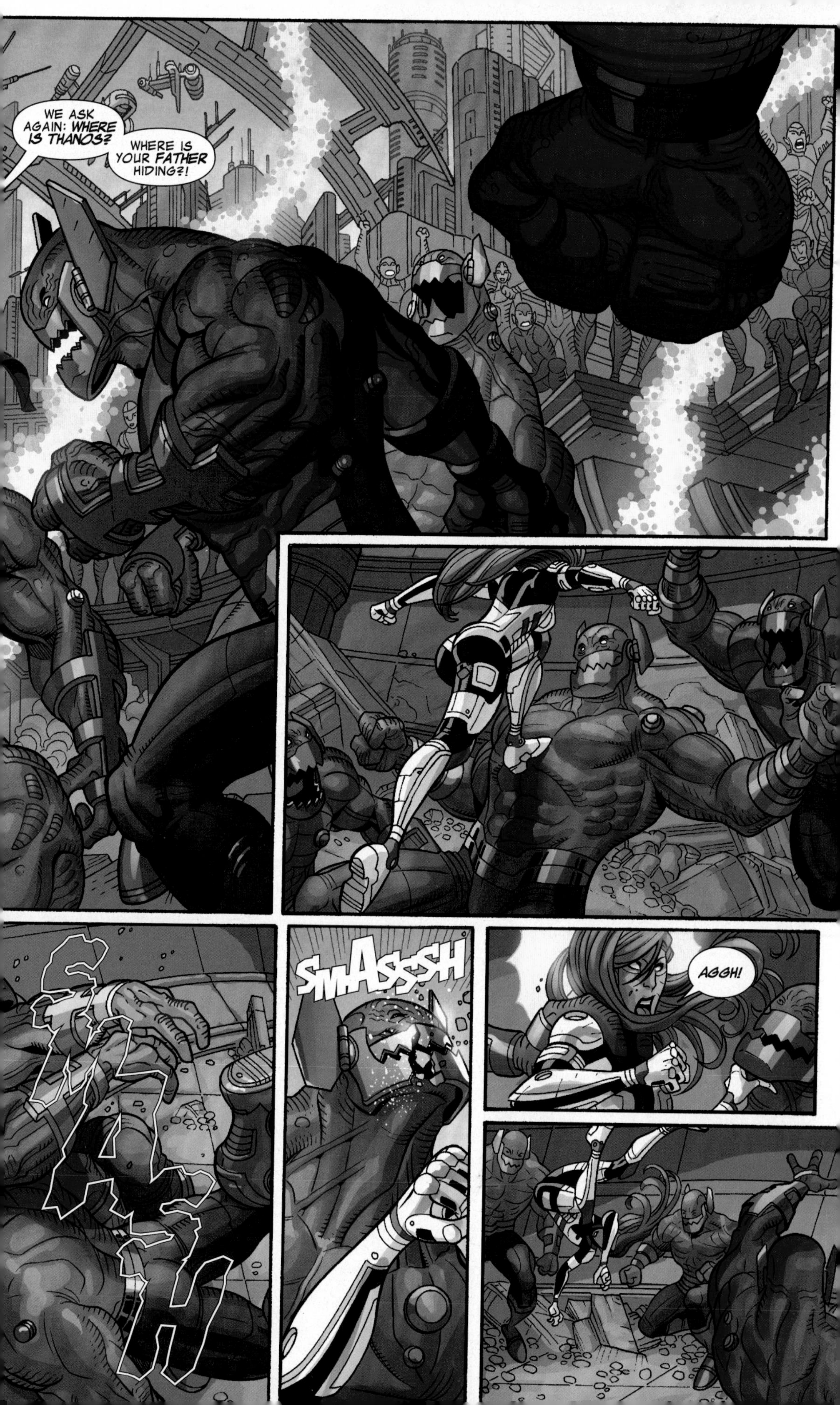
WE ASK AGAIN: WHERE IS THANOS?
WHERE IS YOUR FATHER HIDING?!
SMASSSH
AGGH!

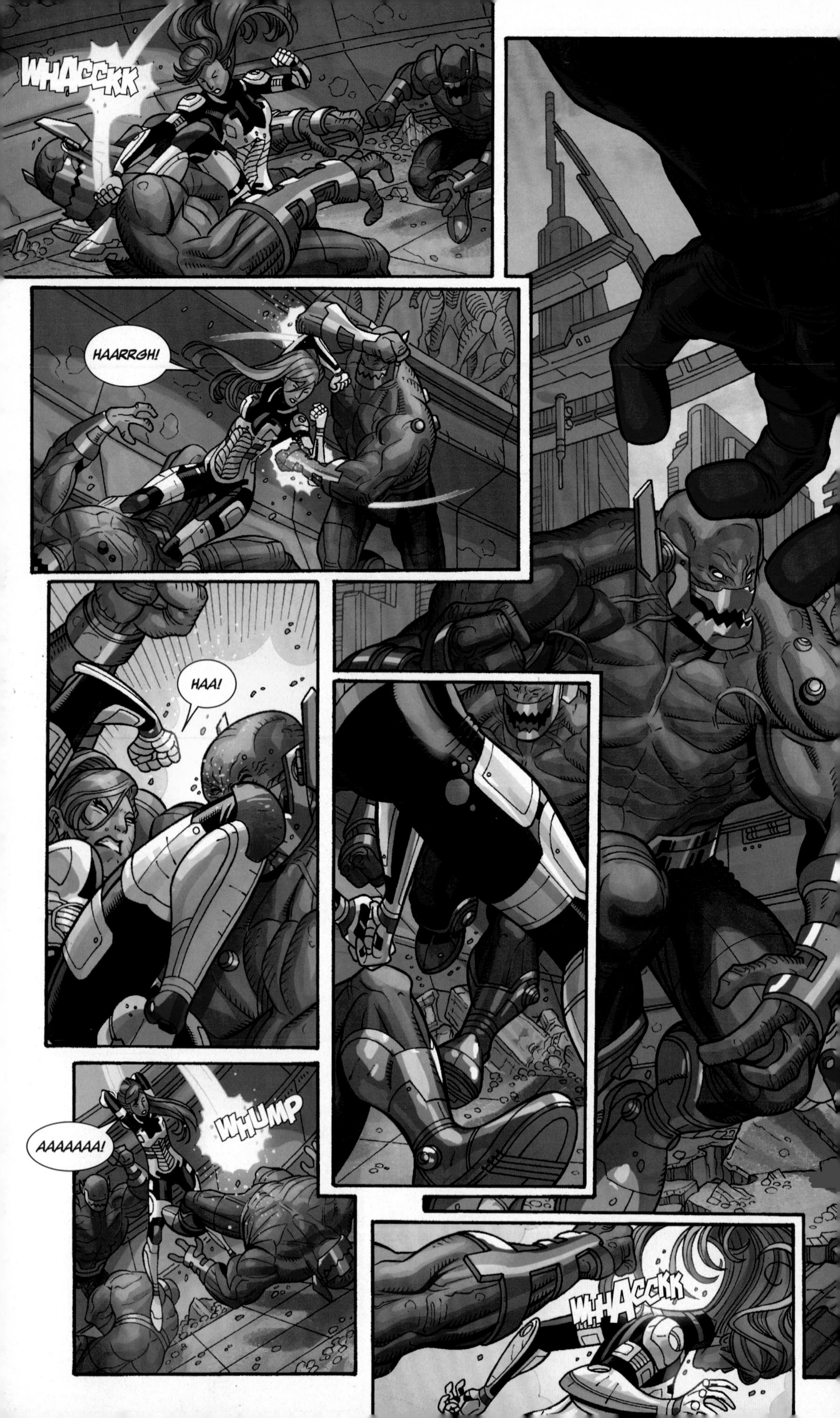
WHACCKK
HAARRGH!
HAA!
AAAAAAA!
WHUMP
WHACCKK

I AM **MANTA** OF THE SHI'AR IMPERIAL GUARD.

I SPEAK NOW FOR THE LEADER AND CHOSEN PRAETOR, GLADIATOR.

ARTHUR SAMPSON DOUGLAS, A.K.A. **DRAX THE DESTROYER**, YOU ARE NOW A PRISONER OF THE SHI'AR EMPIRE.

YOU WILL ANSWER FOR YOUR CRIMES AGAINST THE GALAXY.

YOU WILL ANSWER FOR YOUR NUMEROUS COUNTS OF PIRACY, MURDER, CONSPIRACY...

THAT IS NOT AN APPROPRIATE RESPONSE TO YOUR SITUATION.

YOU ARE A COWARD.

YOU ARE TO BE HELD UNTIL A PROPER TRIAL IS SCHEDULED FOR YOU.

THIS IS ILL-THOUGHT-OUT RETALIATION FOR THE GUARDIANS STOPPING YOUR ILL-THOUGHT-OUT SCHEME TO PUNISH THE EARTH FOR YOUR FAILINGS AS A LEADER.

THE GUARDIANS ARE **NO MORE**.

YOU WI BE **PUNIS** FOR YO CRIME.

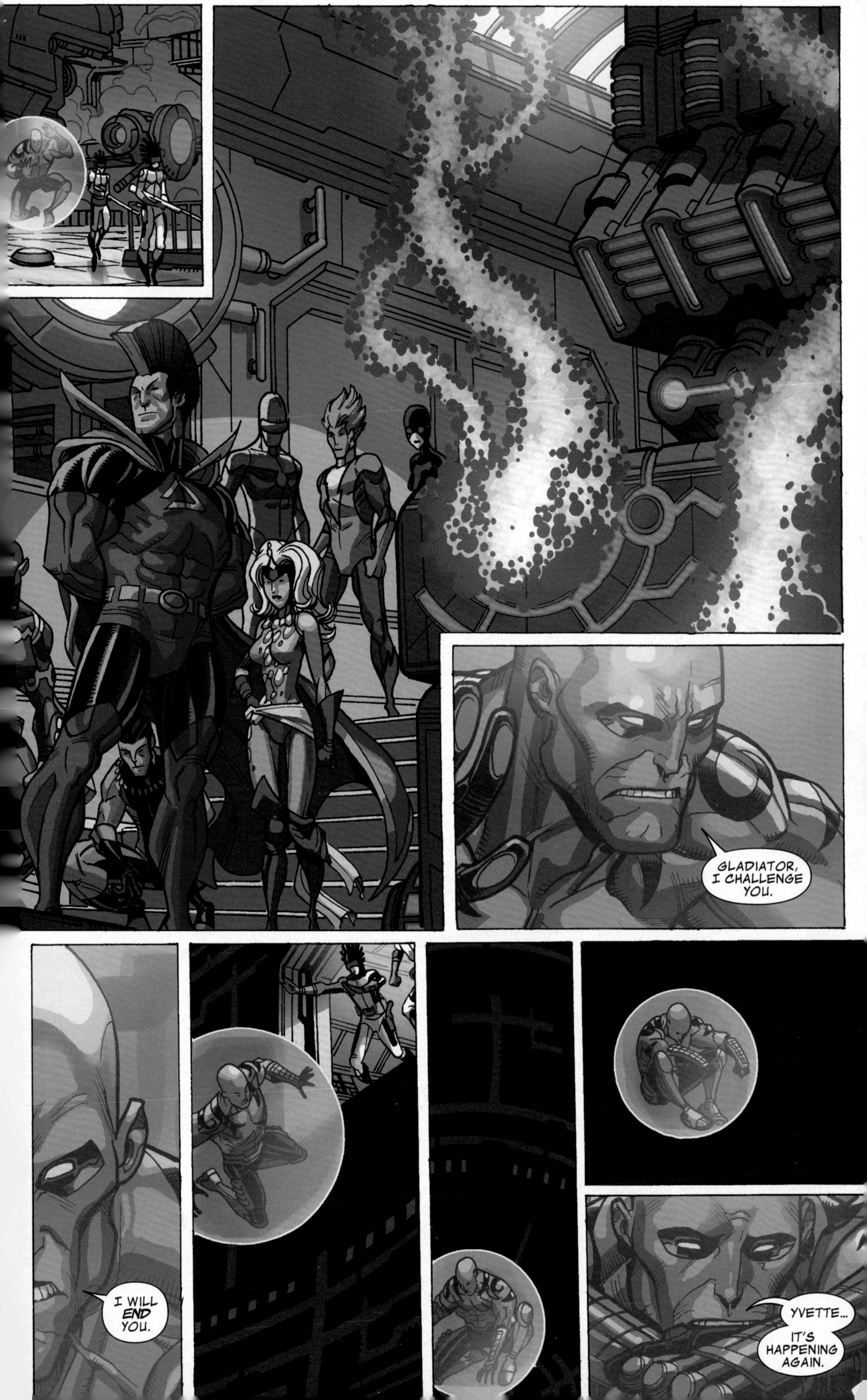
GLADIATOR, I CHALLENGE YOU.
I WILL END YOU.
YVETTE...
IT'S HAPPENING AGAIN.

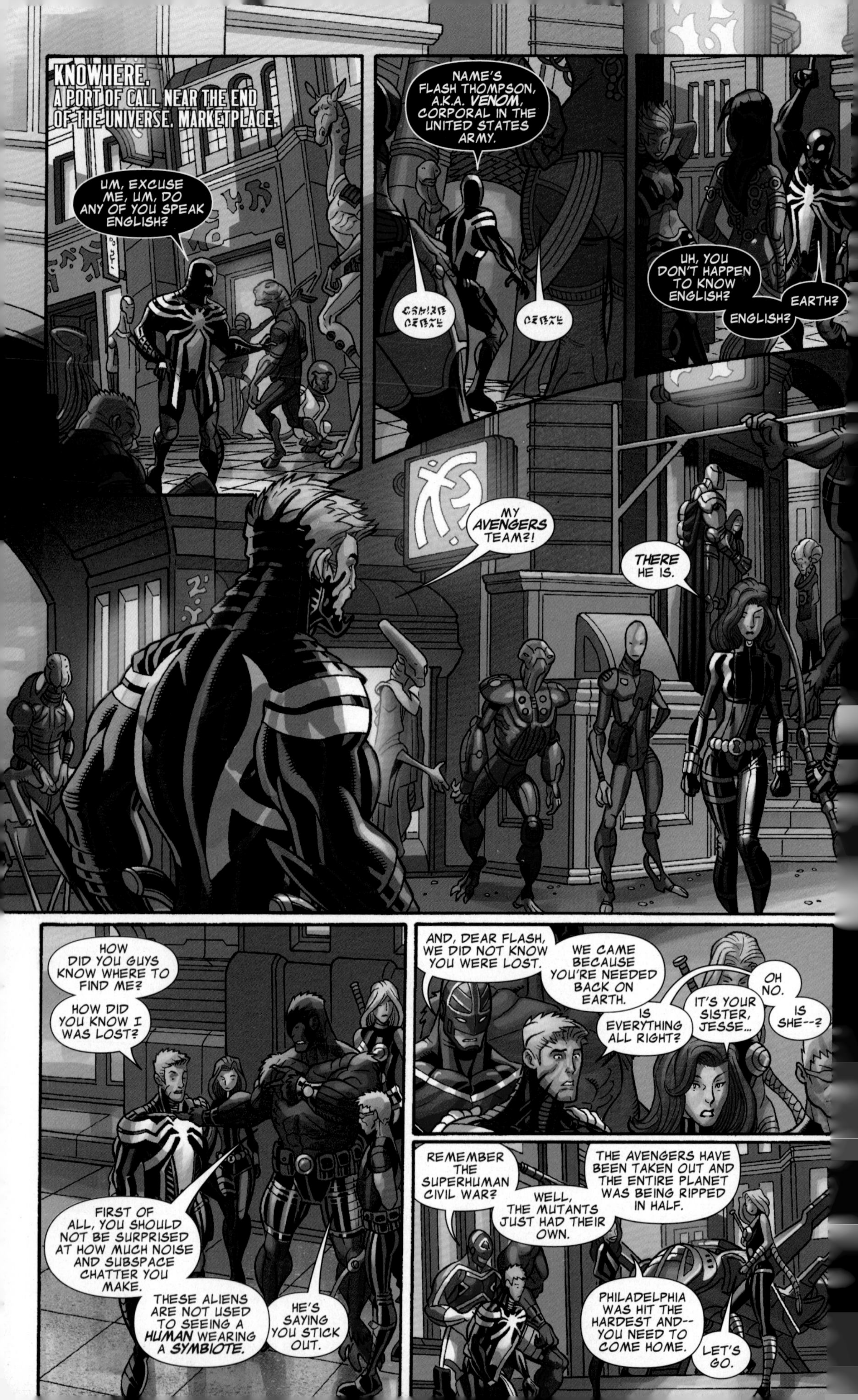
KNOWHERE.
A PORT OF CALL NEAR THE END OF THE UNIVERSE. MARKETPLACE.
UM, EXCUSE ME, UM, DO ANY OF YOU SPEAK ENGLISH?
NAME'S FLASH THOMPSON, A.K.A. VENOM, CORPORAL IN THE UNITED STATES ARMY.
UH, YOU DON'T HAPPEN TO KNOW ENGLISH?
ENGLISH?
EARTH?
MY AVENGERS TEAM?!
THERE HE IS.
HOW DID YOU GUYS KNOW WHERE TO FIND ME?
HOW DID YOU KNOW I WAS LOST?
FIRST OF ALL, YOU SHOULD NOT BE SURPRISED AT HOW MUCH NOISE AND SUBSPACE CHATTER YOU MAKE.
THESE ALIENS ARE NOT USED TO SEEING A HUMAN WEARING A SYMBIOTE.
HE'S SAYING YOU STICK OUT.
AND, DEAR FLASH, WE DID NOT KNOW YOU WERE LOST.
WE CAME BECAUSE YOU'RE NEEDED BACK ON EARTH.
IS EVERYTHING ALL RIGHT?
IT'S YOUR SISTER, JESSE...
OH NO.
IS SHE--?
REMEMBER THE SUPERHUMAN CIVIL WAR?
WELL, THE MUTANTS JUST HAD THEIR OWN.
THE AVENGERS HAVE BEEN TAKEN OUT AND THE ENTIRE PLANET WAS BEING RIPPED IN HALF.
PHILADELPHIA WAS HIT THE HARDEST AND-- YOU NEED TO COME HOME.
LET'S GO.

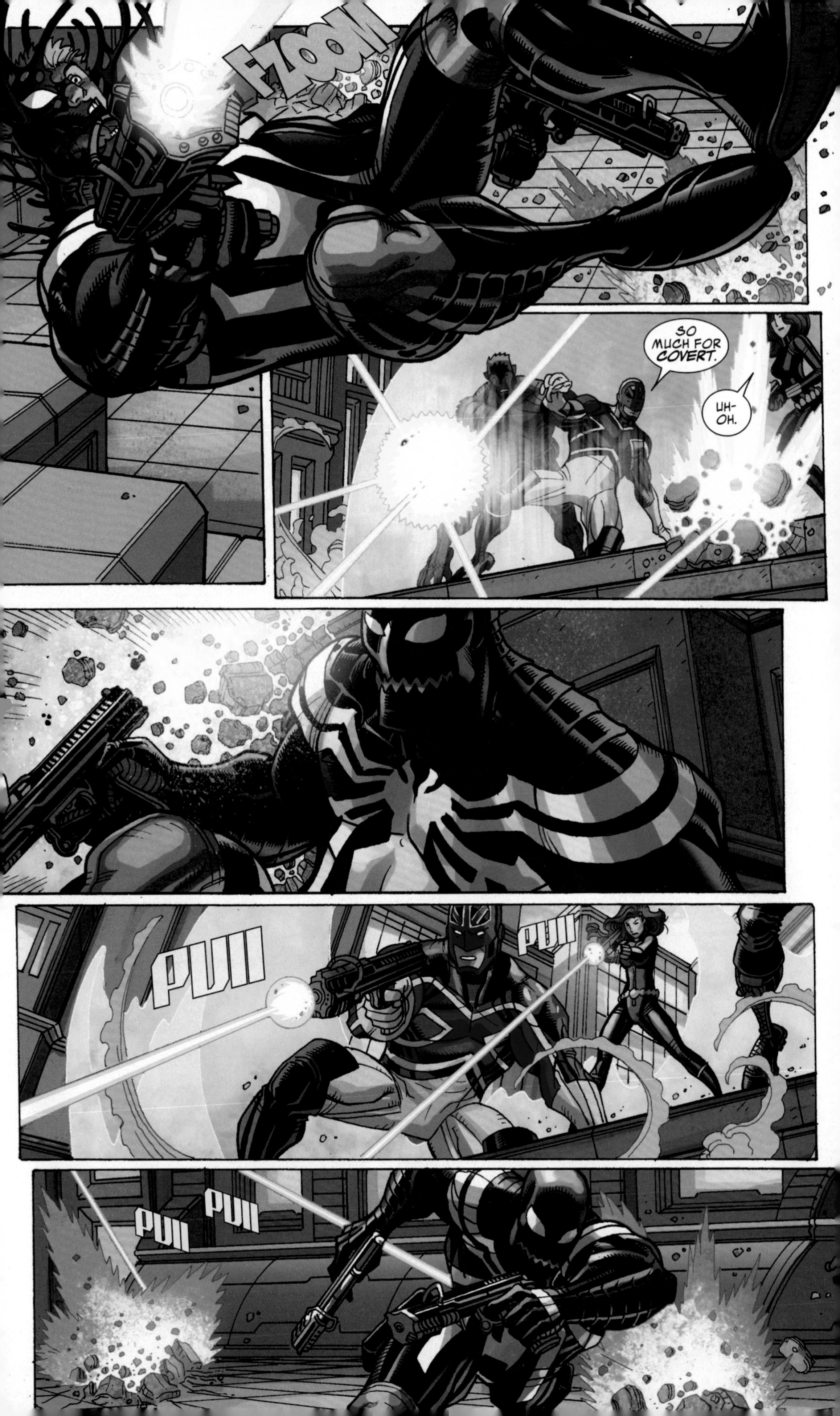
FZOOM
SO MUCH FOR COVERT.
UH-OH.
PUII
PUII
PUII
PUII

PUII
PUII
PUII
PUII
PUII

SLIPPERY.

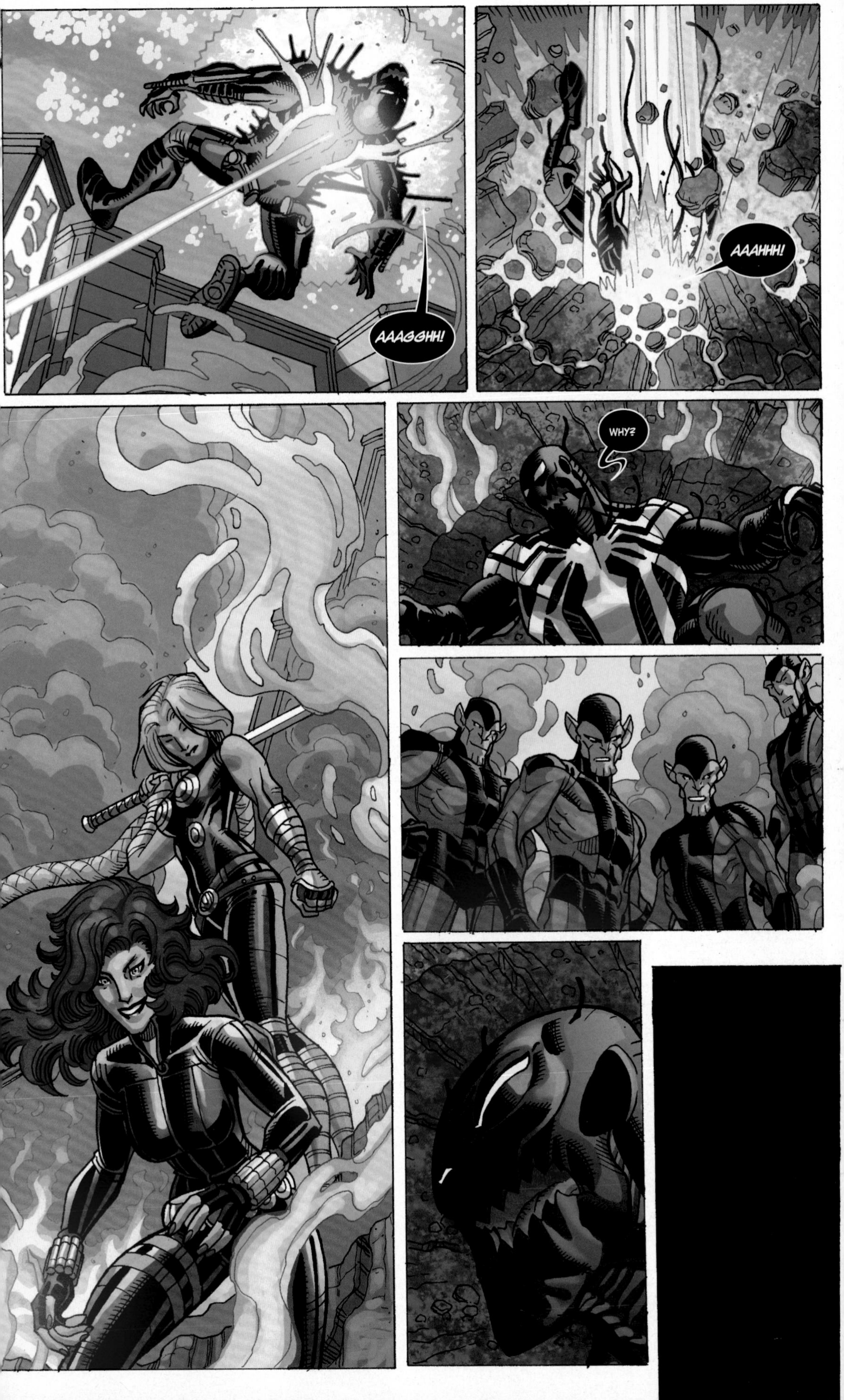
AAAGGHH!
AAAHHH!
WHY?

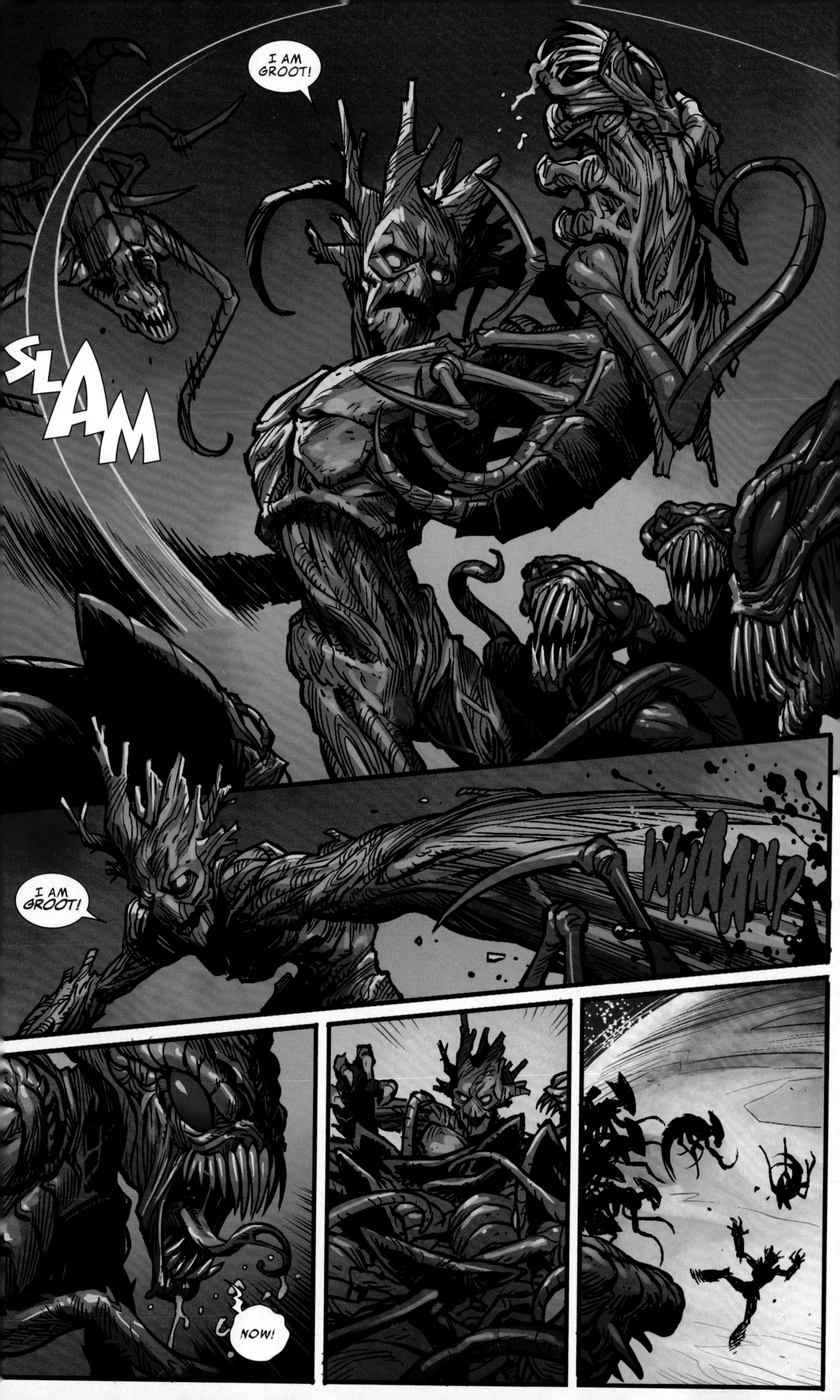
I AM GROOT!
SLAM
I AM GROOT!
WHAAMP
NOW!

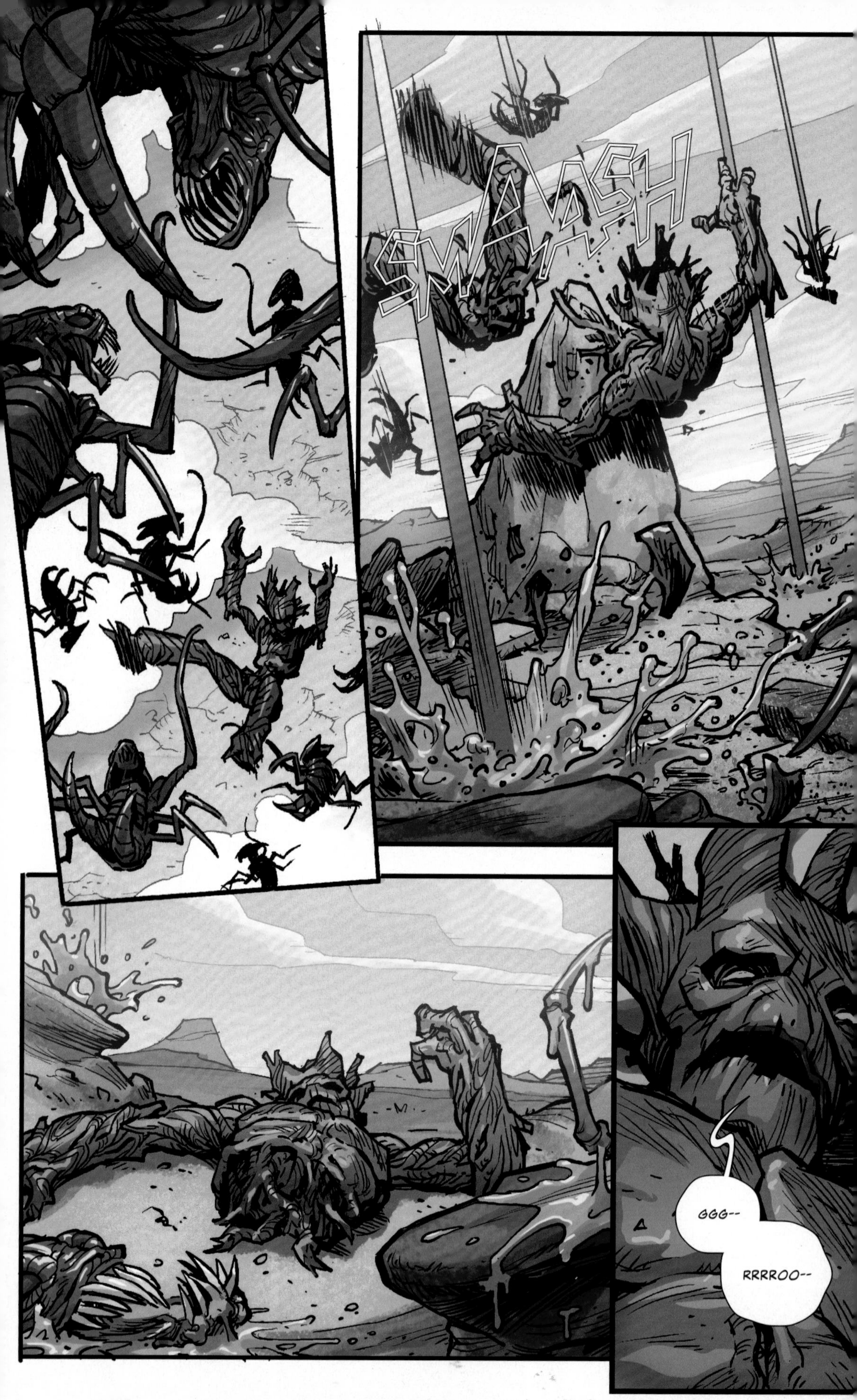
SWAASH
GGG--
RRRROO--

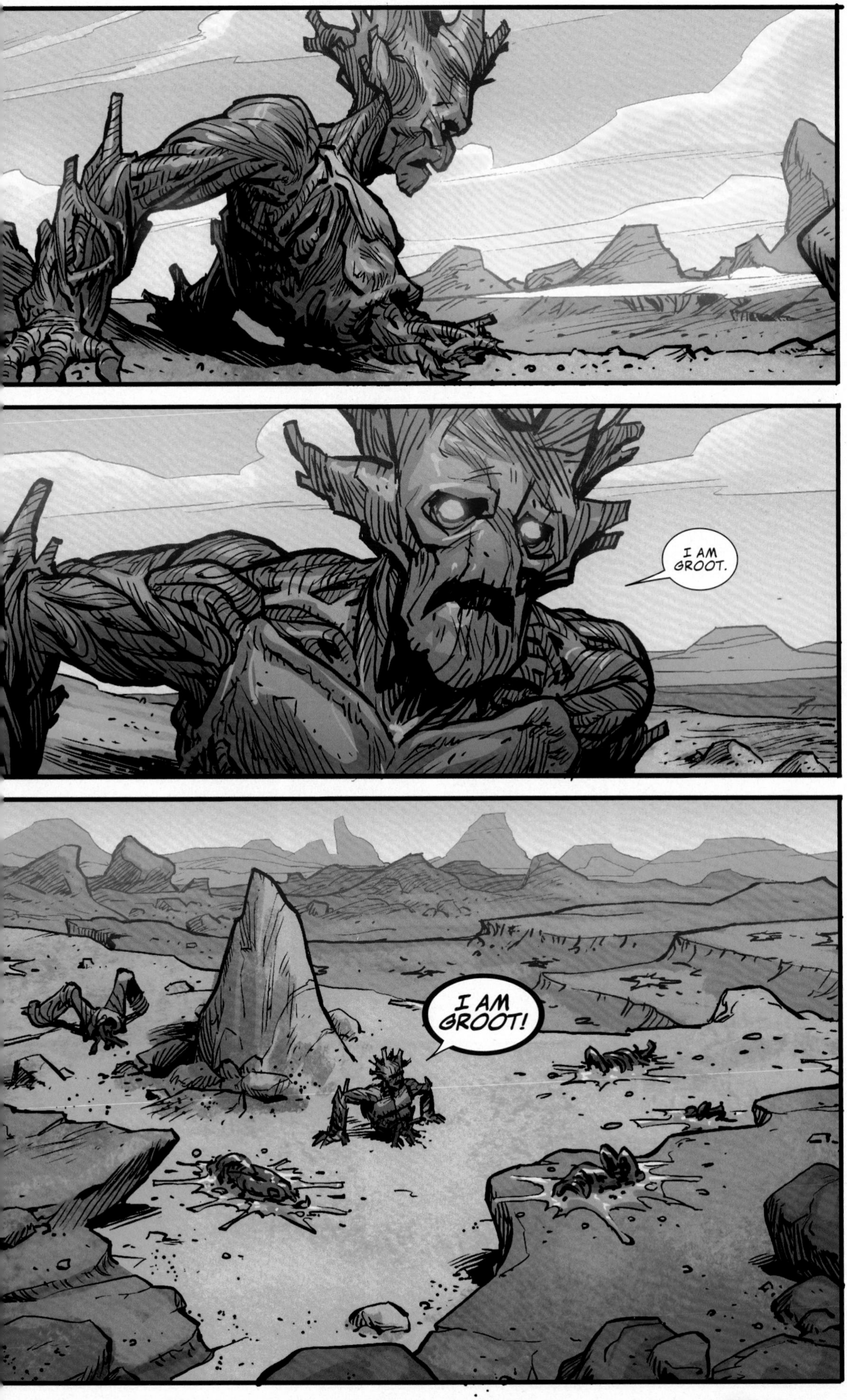
I AM GROOT.
I AM GROOT!

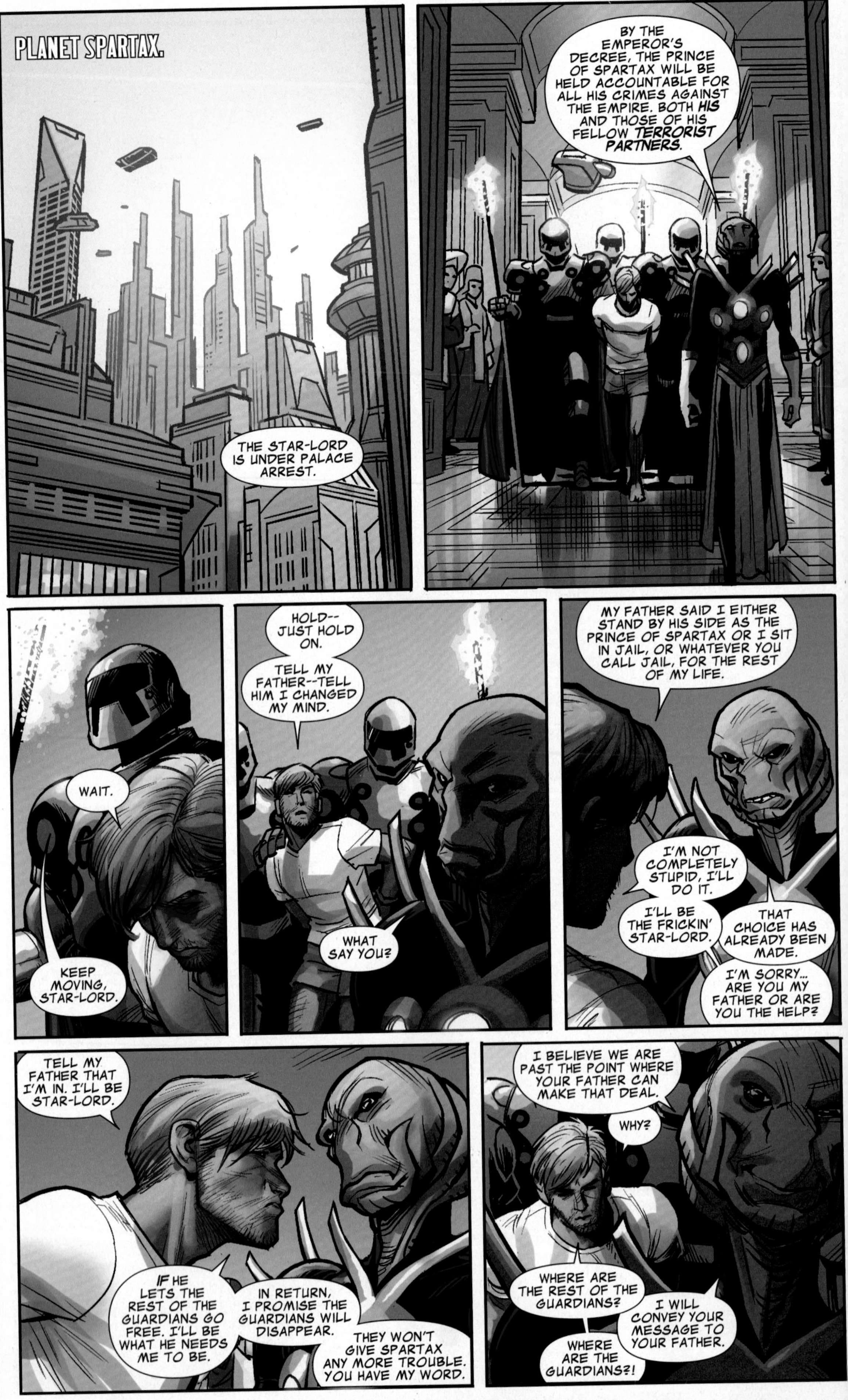
PLANET SPARTAX.
THE STAR-LORD IS UNDER PALACE ARREST.
BY THE EMPEROR'S DECREE, THE PRINCE OF SPARTAX WILL BE HELD ACCOUNTABLE FOR ALL HIS CRIMES AGAINST THE EMPIRE. BOTH HIS AND THOSE OF HIS FELLOW TERRORIST PARTNERS.
WAIT.
KEEP MOVING, STAR-LORD.
HOLD--JUST HOLD ON.
TELL MY FATHER--TELL HIM I CHANGED MY MIND.
WHAT SAY YOU?
MY FATHER SAID I EITHER STAND BY HIS SIDE AS THE PRINCE OF SPARTAX OR I SIT IN JAIL, OR WHATEVER YOU CALL JAIL, FOR THE REST OF MY LIFE.
I'M NOT COMPLETELY STUPID, I'LL DO IT.
I'LL BE THE FRICKIN' STAR-LORD.
THAT CHOICE HAS ALREADY BEEN MADE.
I'M SORRY... ARE YOU MY FATHER OR ARE YOU THE HELP?
TELL MY FATHER THAT I'M IN. I'LL BE STAR-LORD.
IF HE LETS THE REST OF THE GUARDIANS GO FREE. I'LL BE WHAT HE NEEDS ME TO BE.
IN RETURN, I PROMISE THE GUARDIANS WILL DISAPPEAR.
THEY WON'T GIVE SPARTAX ANY MORE TROUBLE. YOU HAVE MY WORD.
I BELIEVE WE ARE PAST THE POINT WHERE YOUR FATHER CAN MAKE THAT DEAL.
WHY?
WHERE ARE THE REST OF THE GUARDIANS?
I WILL CONVEY YOUR MESSAGE TO YOUR FATHER.
WHERE ARE THE GUARDIANS?!

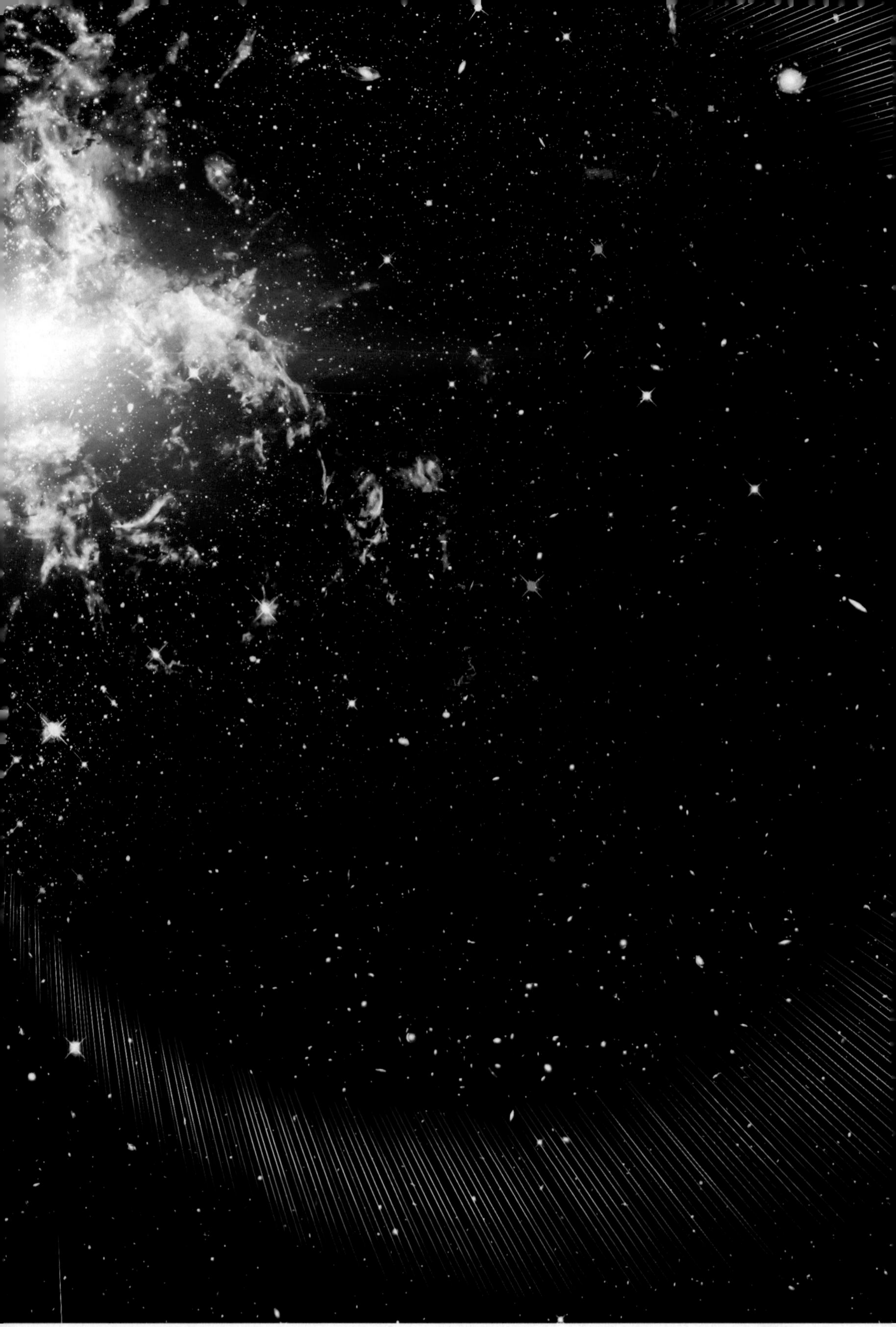

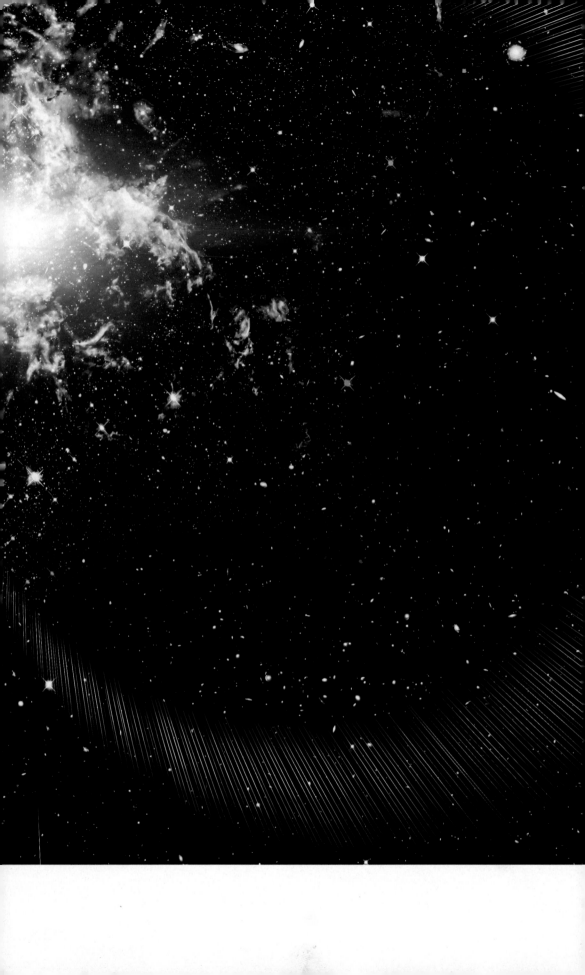

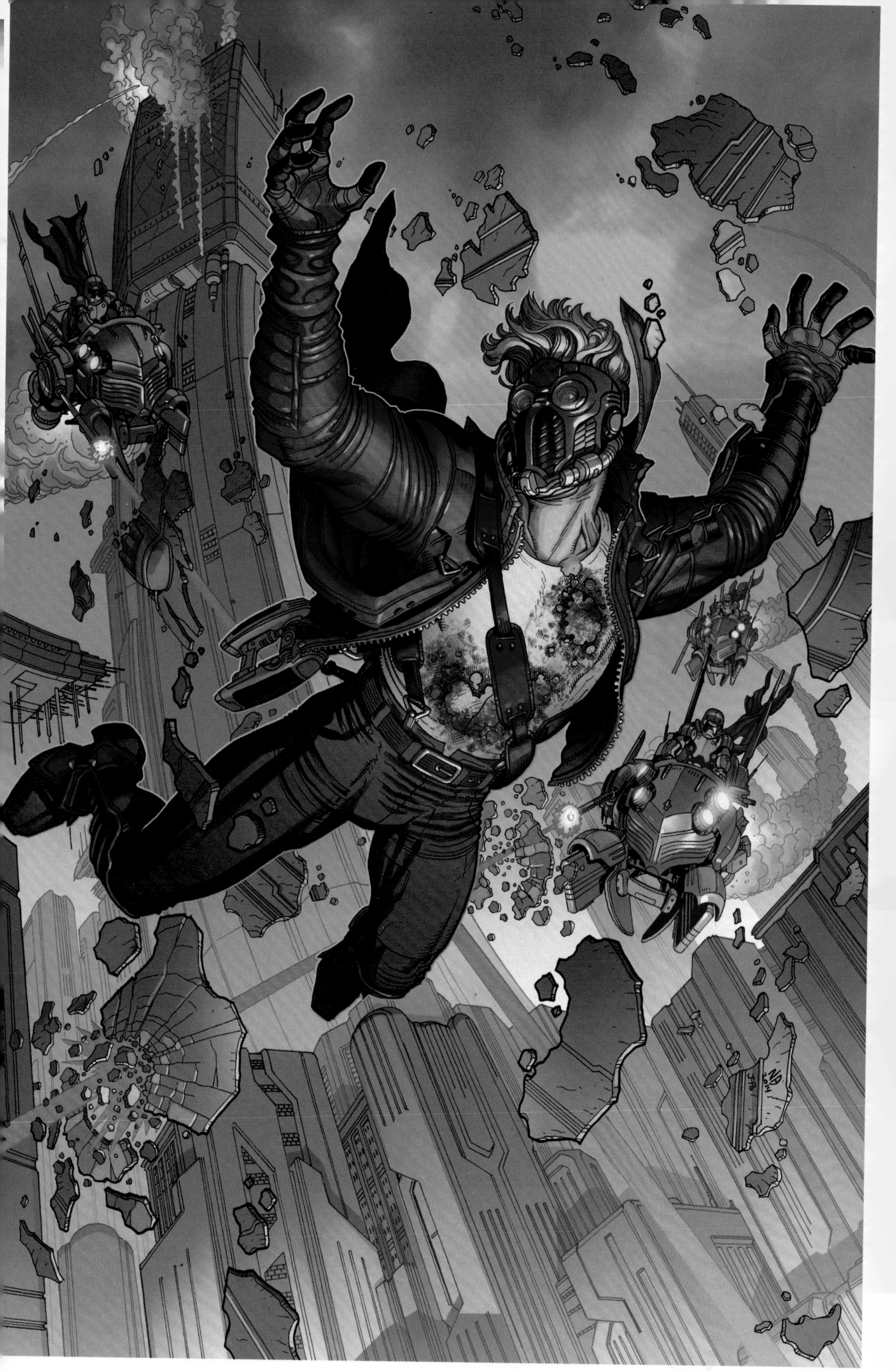

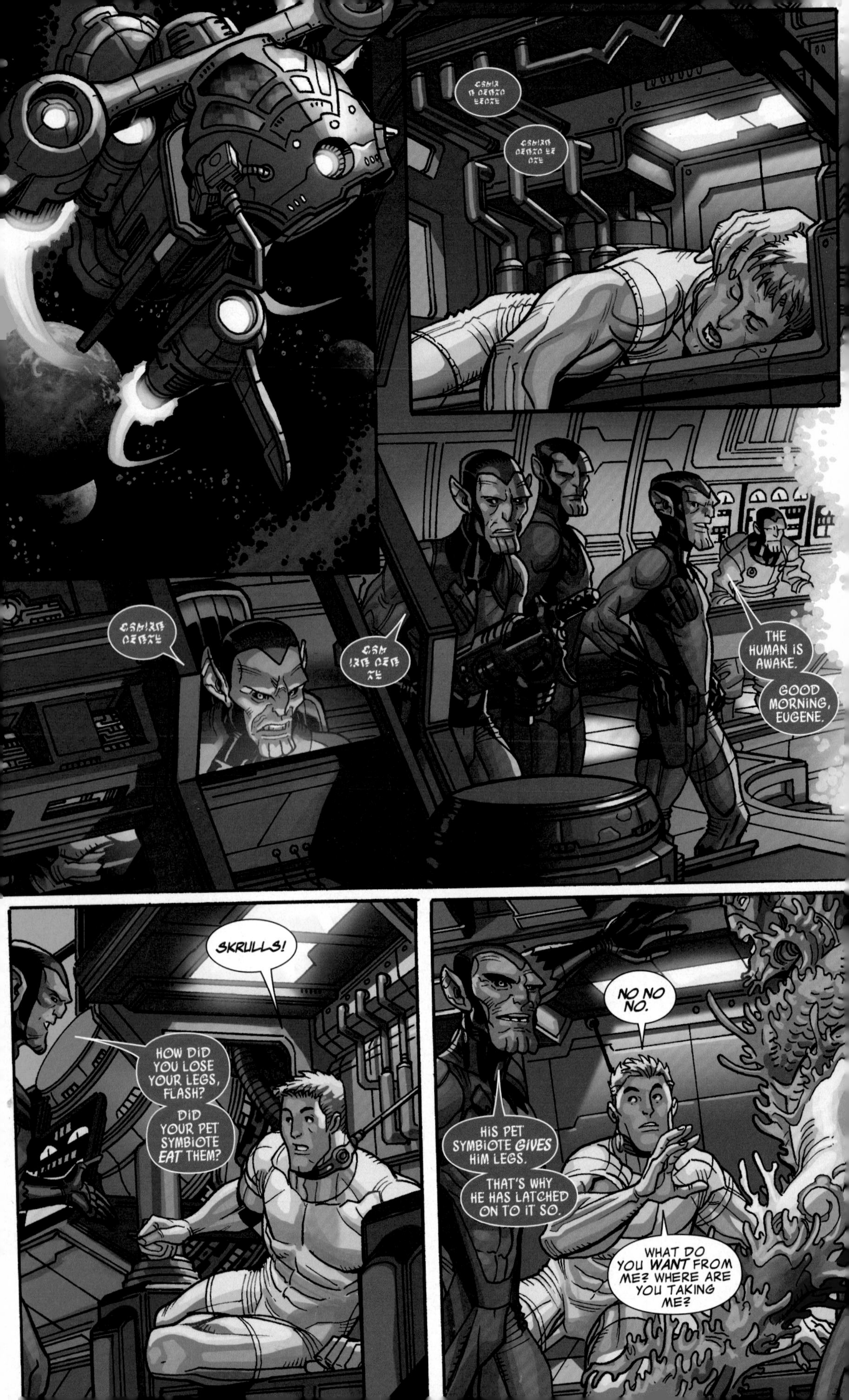
THE HUMAN IS AWAKE.
GOOD MORNING, EUGENE.
SKRULLS!
HOW DID YOU LOSE YOUR LEGS, FLASH?
DID YOUR PET SYMBIOTE EAT THEM?
NO NO NO.
HIS PET SYMBIOTE GIVES HIM LEGS.
THAT'S WHY HE HAS LATCHED ON TO IT SO.
WHAT DO YOU WANT FROM ME? WHERE ARE YOU TAKING ME?

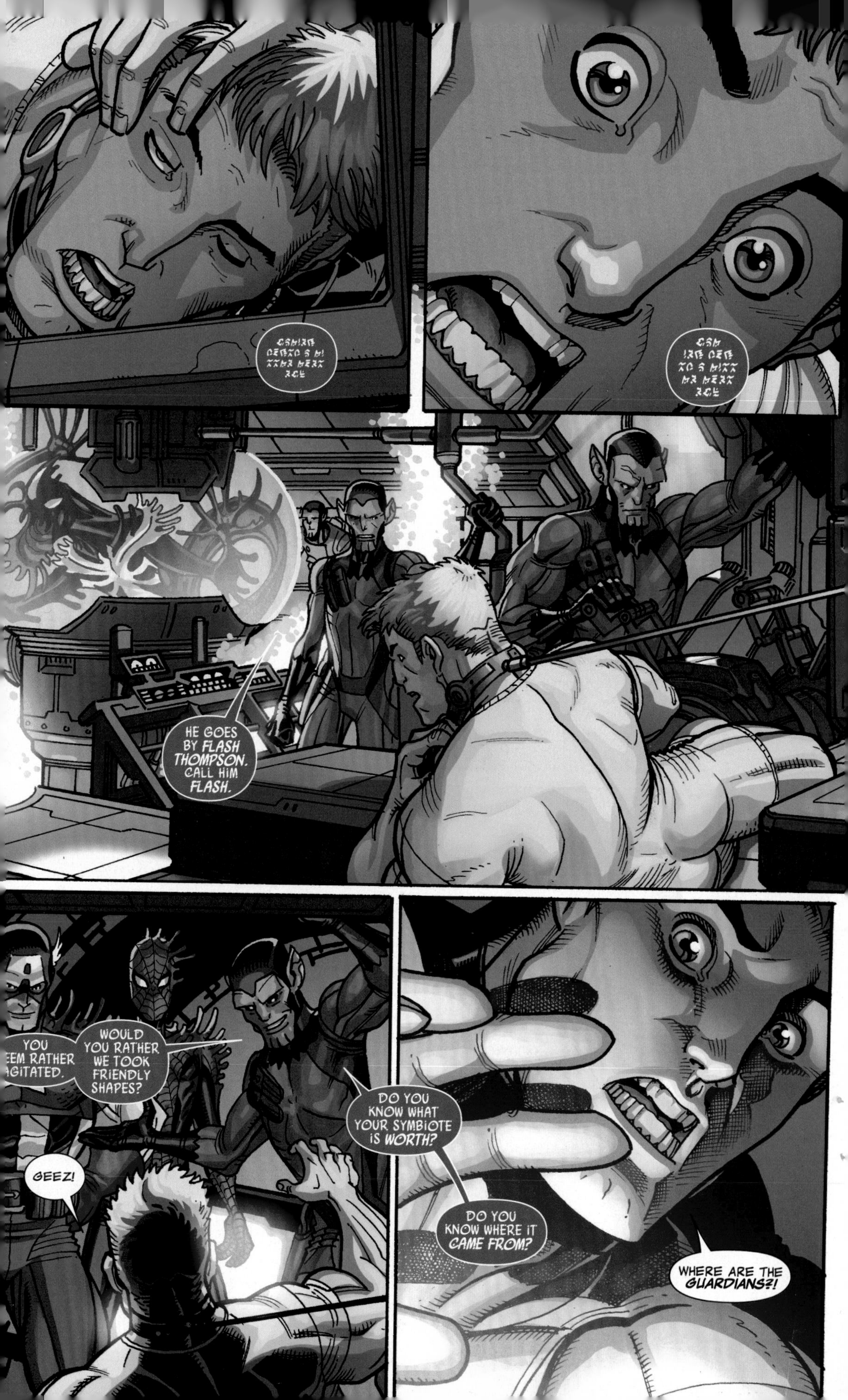
HE GOES BY FLASH THOMPSON. CALL HIM FLASH.
YOU EEM RATHER AGITATED.
WOULD YOU RATHER WE TOOK FRIENDLY SHAPES?
DO YOU KNOW WHAT YOUR SYMBIOTE IS WORTH?
GEEZ!
DO YOU KNOW WHERE IT CAME FROM?
WHERE ARE THE GUARDIANS?!

THE IMPERIUM TRIBUNAL WILL NOW BE SILENT, FOR WE ARE ABOUT TO BEGIN!

THIS HUMAN WAS TRANSFORMED INTO THIS--THIS SO-CALLED "DESTROYER"-- FOR THE SOLE PURPOSE OF ATTACKING AND KILLING THE MAD TITAN *THANOS.*

BUT INSTEAD HE HAS CHOSEN TO USE HIS GIFTS FOR TERRORISM AND THIEVERY.

ALL THIS IS *FACT.*

BUT HE IS HERE TO ANSWER FOR HIS PART IN OBSTRUCTING OUR WAY OF JUSTICE AND HIS ALLIANCE WITH THE EARTH PHOENIX VESSEL KNOWN AS *JEAN GREY.*

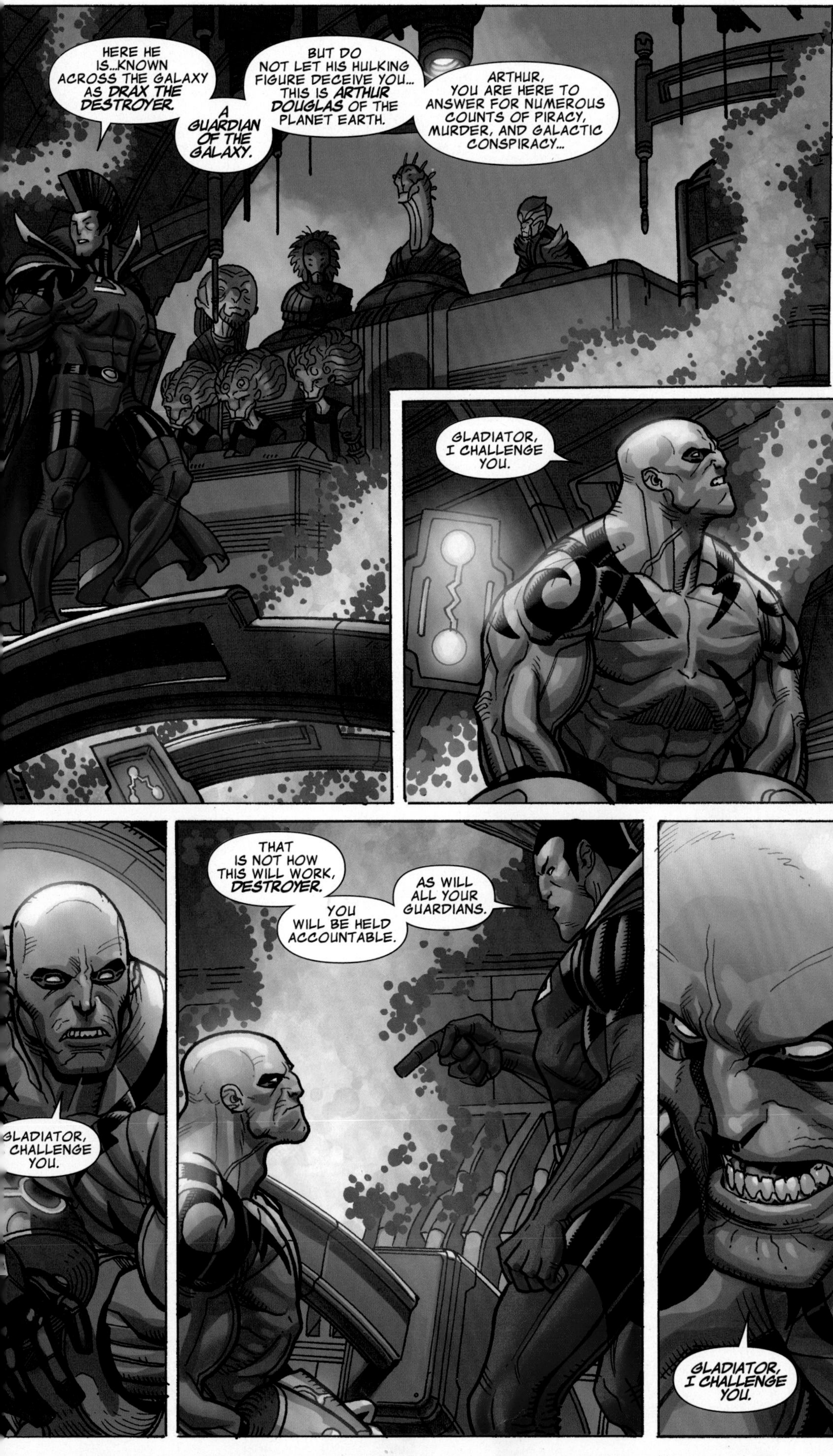

HERE HE IS...KNOWN ACROSS THE GALAXY AS DRAX THE DESTROYER.
A GUARDIAN OF THE GALAXY.
BUT DO NOT LET HIS HULKING FIGURE DECEIVE YOU... THIS IS ARTHUR DOUGLAS OF THE PLANET EARTH.
ARTHUR, YOU ARE HERE TO ANSWER FOR NUMEROUS COUNTS OF PIRACY, MURDER, AND GALACTIC CONSPIRACY...
GLADIATOR, I CHALLENGE YOU.
GLADIATOR, CHALLENGE YOU.
THAT IS NOT HOW THIS WILL WORK, DESTROYER.
YOU WILL BE HELD ACCOUNTABLE.
AS WILL ALL YOUR GUARDIANS.
GLADIATOR, I CHALLENGE YOU.

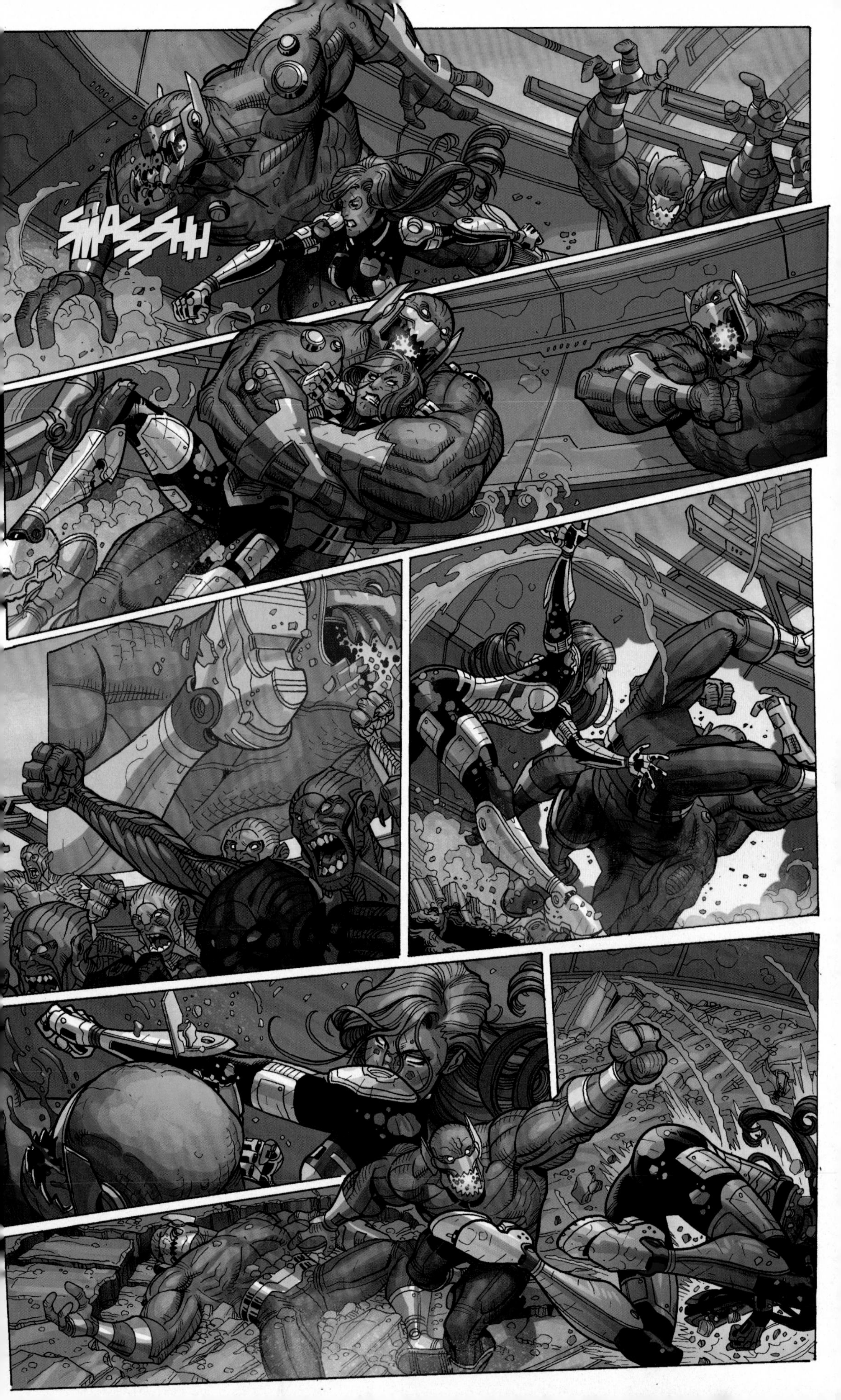
SMASSHH

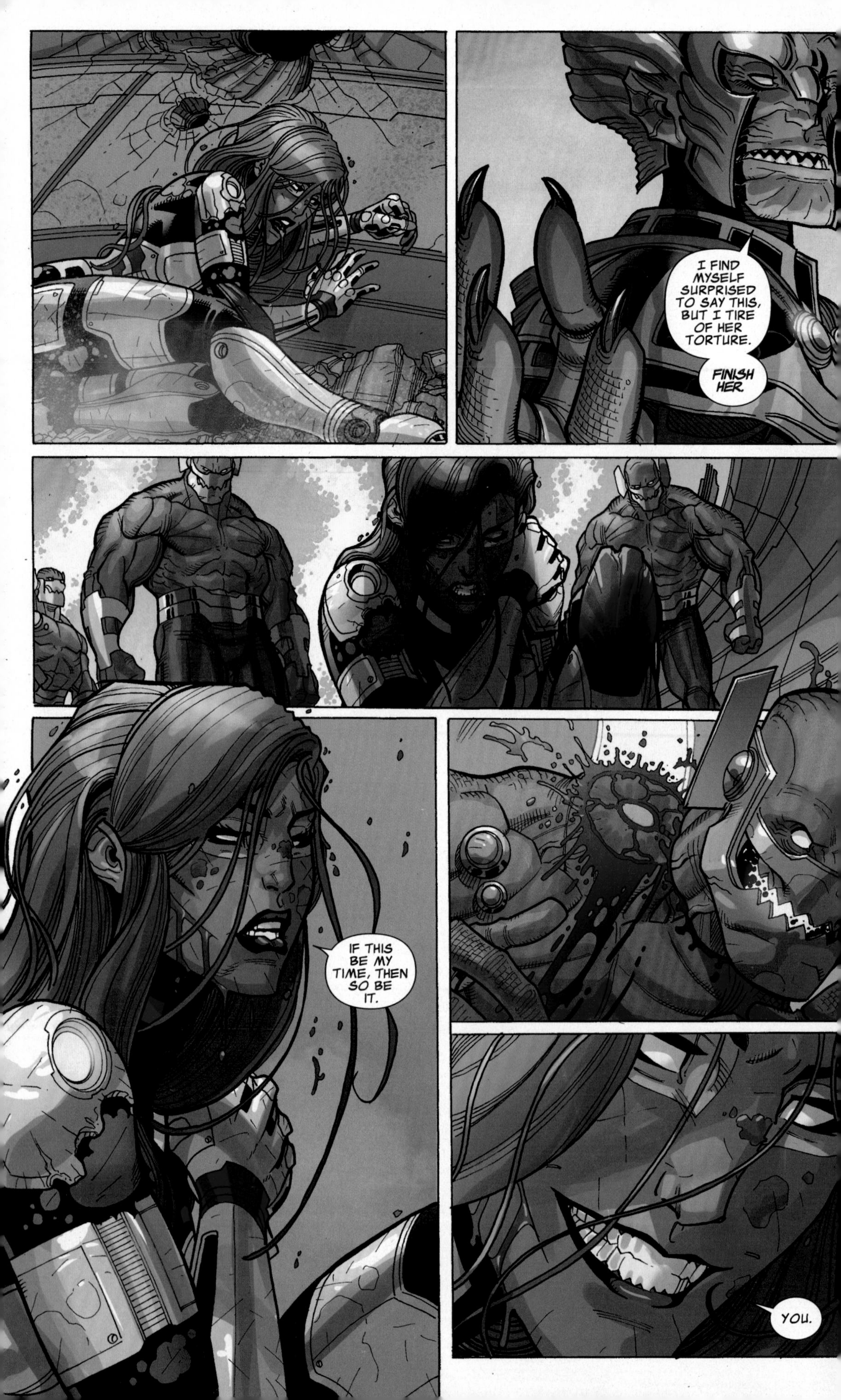

I FIND MYSELF SURPRISED TO SAY THIS, BUT I TIRE OF HER TORTURE.
FINISH HER.
IF THIS BE MY TIME, THEN SO BE IT.
YOU.

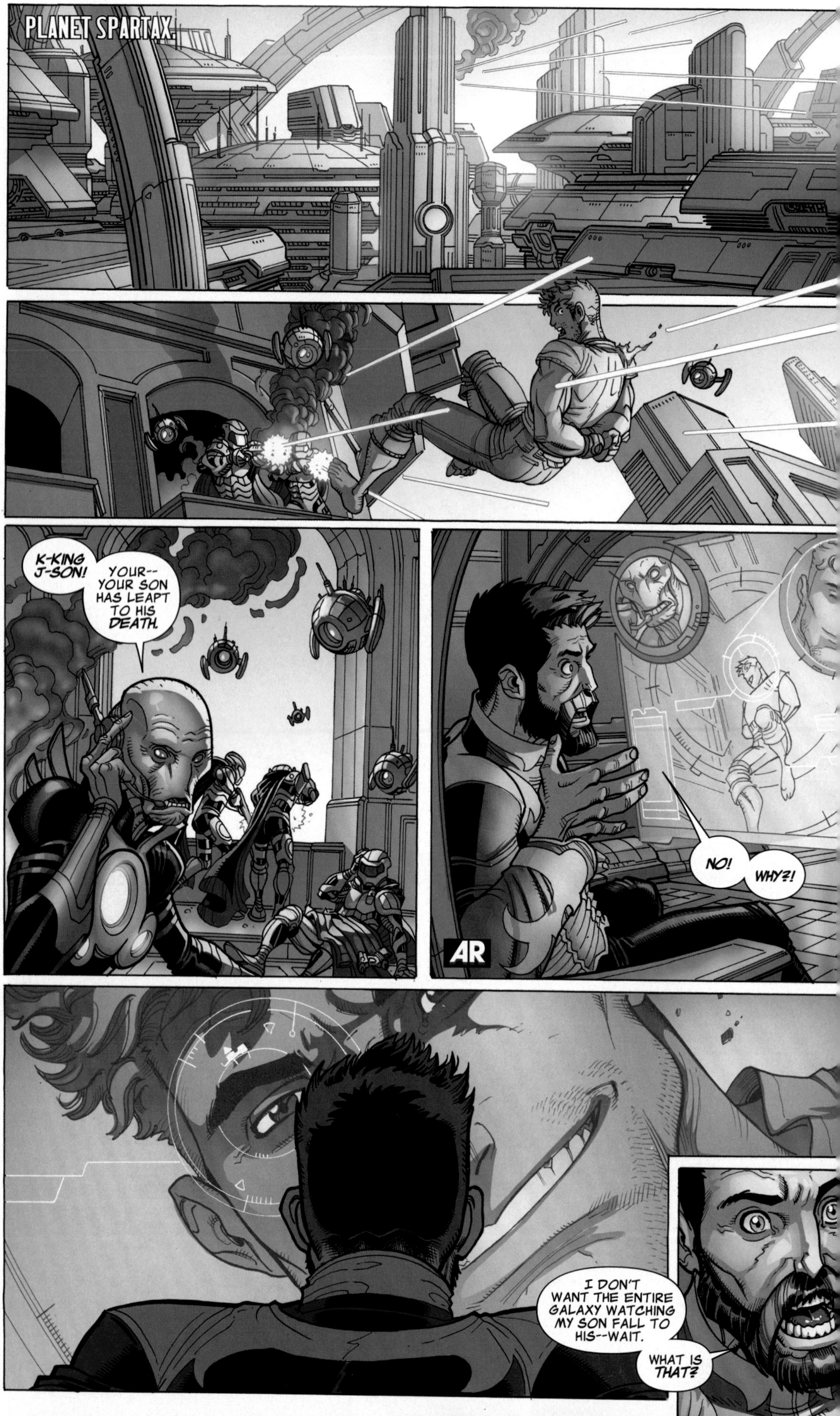
PLANET SPARTAX.
K-KING J-SON!
YOUR-- YOUR SON HAS LEAPT TO HIS DEATH.
NO!
WHY?!
I DON'T WANT THE ENTIRE GALAXY WATCHING MY SON FALL TO HIS--WAIT.
WHAT IS THAT?

ZZZAAATKKKTTT

THE GUN IS SET TO ME AND ME ONLY, GENIUS.

I'M THE FRICKIN' STAR-LORD AND YOU'RE A SPARTAX ROYAL GUARD.

YOU SHOULD HAVE KNOWN THAT.

FSSHHAAMM

LET'S GET YOUR STUFF AND GET OUT OF HERE!

GO FIND THE OTHER GUARDIANS.

NUH-UH. NOT YET.

HI.

WHERE ARE THE OTHER GUARDIANS OF THE GALAXY?

AND MY PANTS?

YOU--YOU'LL HAVE TO A-ASK YOUR FATHER.

I'M ASKING YOU.

WHAT DID YOU DO TO THE GUARDIANS?

STAND DOWN, STAR-LORD!

I TOLD YOU!

THE GUARDIANS ARE NO MORE!

HEY, DAD...

I AM THE KING OF SPARTAX AND I WILL NOT HAVE THIS INCURSION!

YOU ARE SHAMING THIS HOUSE!

YOU ARE DESECRATING YOUR BLOODLINE!

REALLY?

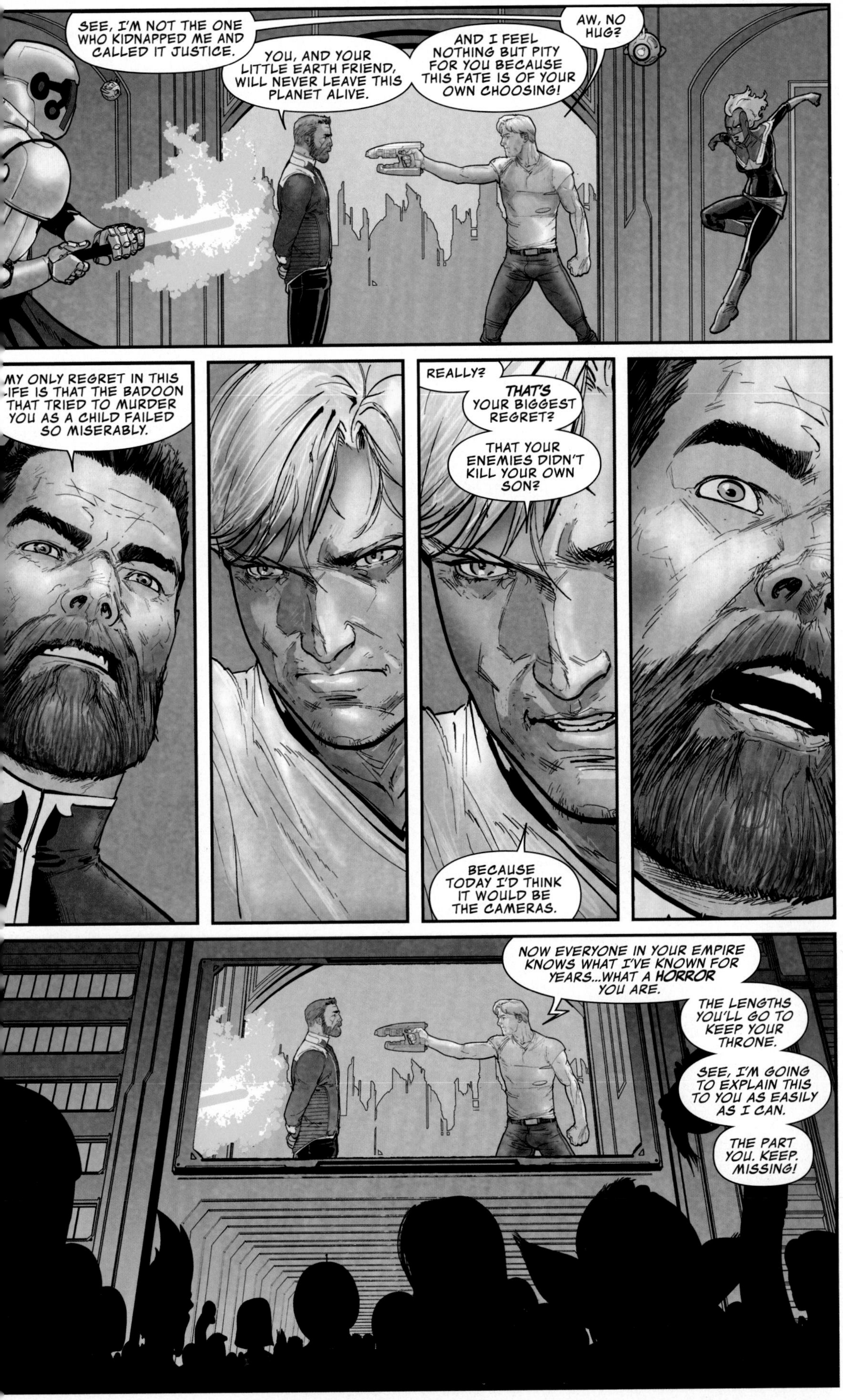
SEE, I'M NOT THE ONE WHO KIDNAPPED ME AND CALLED IT JUSTICE.
YOU, AND YOUR LITTLE EARTH FRIEND, WILL NEVER LEAVE THIS PLANET ALIVE.
AND I FEEL NOTHING BUT PITY FOR YOU BECAUSE THIS FATE IS OF YOUR OWN CHOOSING!
AW, NO HUG?
MY ONLY REGRET IN THIS LIFE IS THAT THE BADOON THAT TRIED TO MURDER YOU AS A CHILD FAILED SO MISERABLY.
REALLY?
THAT'S YOUR BIGGEST REGRET?
THAT YOUR ENEMIES DIDN'T KILL YOUR OWN SON?
BECAUSE TODAY I'D THINK IT WOULD BE THE CAMERAS.
NOW EVERYONE IN YOUR EMPIRE KNOWS WHAT I'VE KNOWN FOR YEARS...WHAT A HORROR YOU ARE.
THE LENGTHS YOU'LL GO TO KEEP YOUR THRONE.
SEE, I'M GOING TO EXPLAIN THIS TO YOU AS EASILY AS I CAN.
THE PART YOU. KEEP. MISSING!

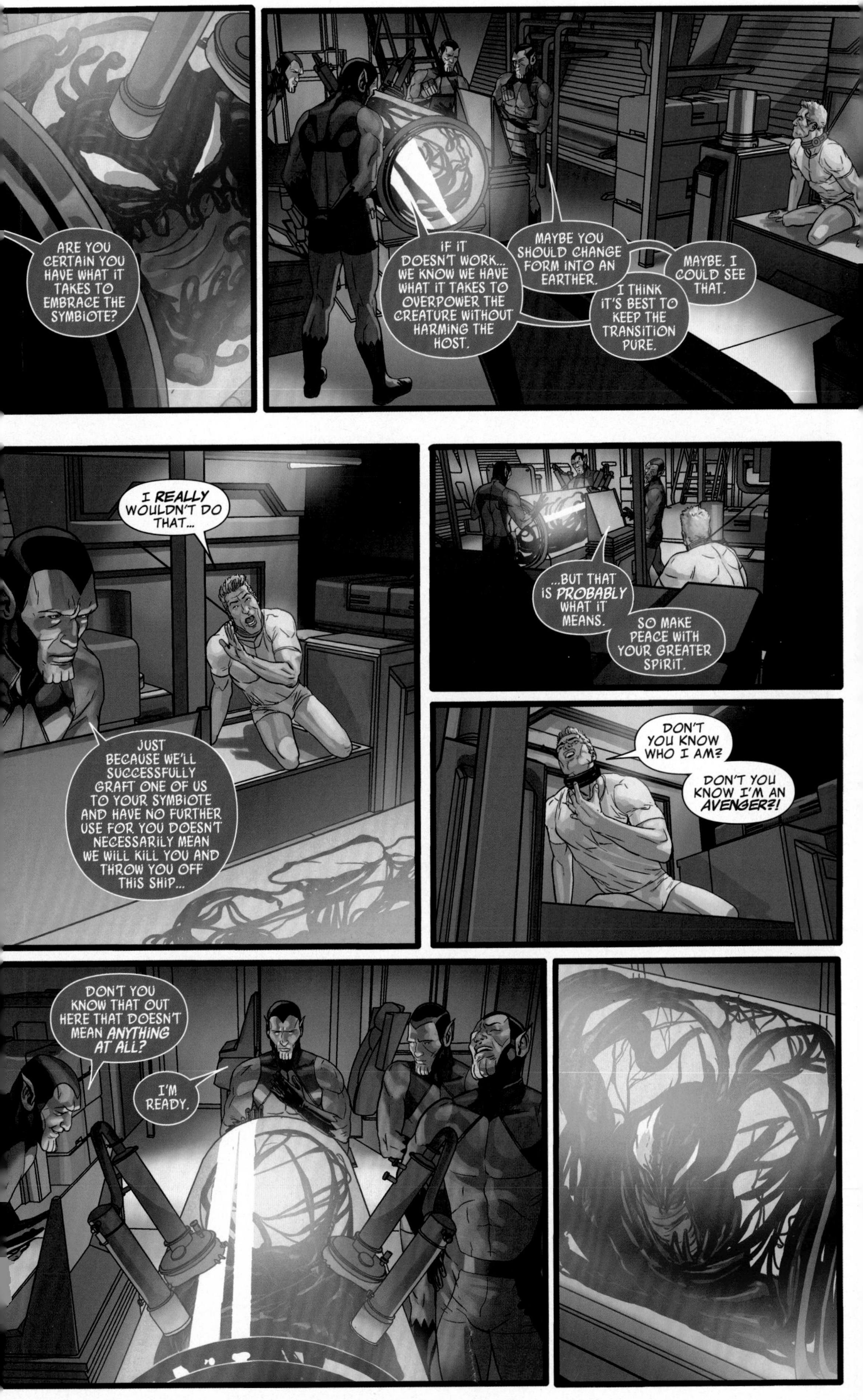
ARE YOU CERTAIN YOU HAVE WHAT IT TAKES TO EMBRACE THE SYMBIOTE?
IF IT DOESN'T WORK... WE KNOW WE HAVE WHAT IT TAKES TO OVERPOWER THE CREATURE WITHOUT HARMING THE HOST.
MAYBE YOU SHOULD CHANGE FORM INTO AN EARTHER.
I THINK IT'S BEST TO KEEP THE TRANSITION PURE.
MAYBE. I COULD SEE THAT.
I REALLY WOULDN'T DO THAT...
JUST BECAUSE WE'LL SUCCESSFULLY GRAFT ONE OF US TO YOUR SYMBIOTE AND HAVE NO FURTHER USE FOR YOU DOESN'T NECESSARILY MEAN WE WILL KILL YOU AND THROW YOU OFF THIS SHIP...
...BUT THAT IS PROBABLY WHAT IT MEANS.
SO MAKE PEACE WITH YOUR GREATER SPIRIT.
DON'T YOU KNOW WHO I AM?
DON'T YOU KNOW I'M AN AVENGER?!
DON'T YOU KNOW THAT OUT HERE THAT DOESN'T MEAN ANYTHING AT ALL?
I'M READY.

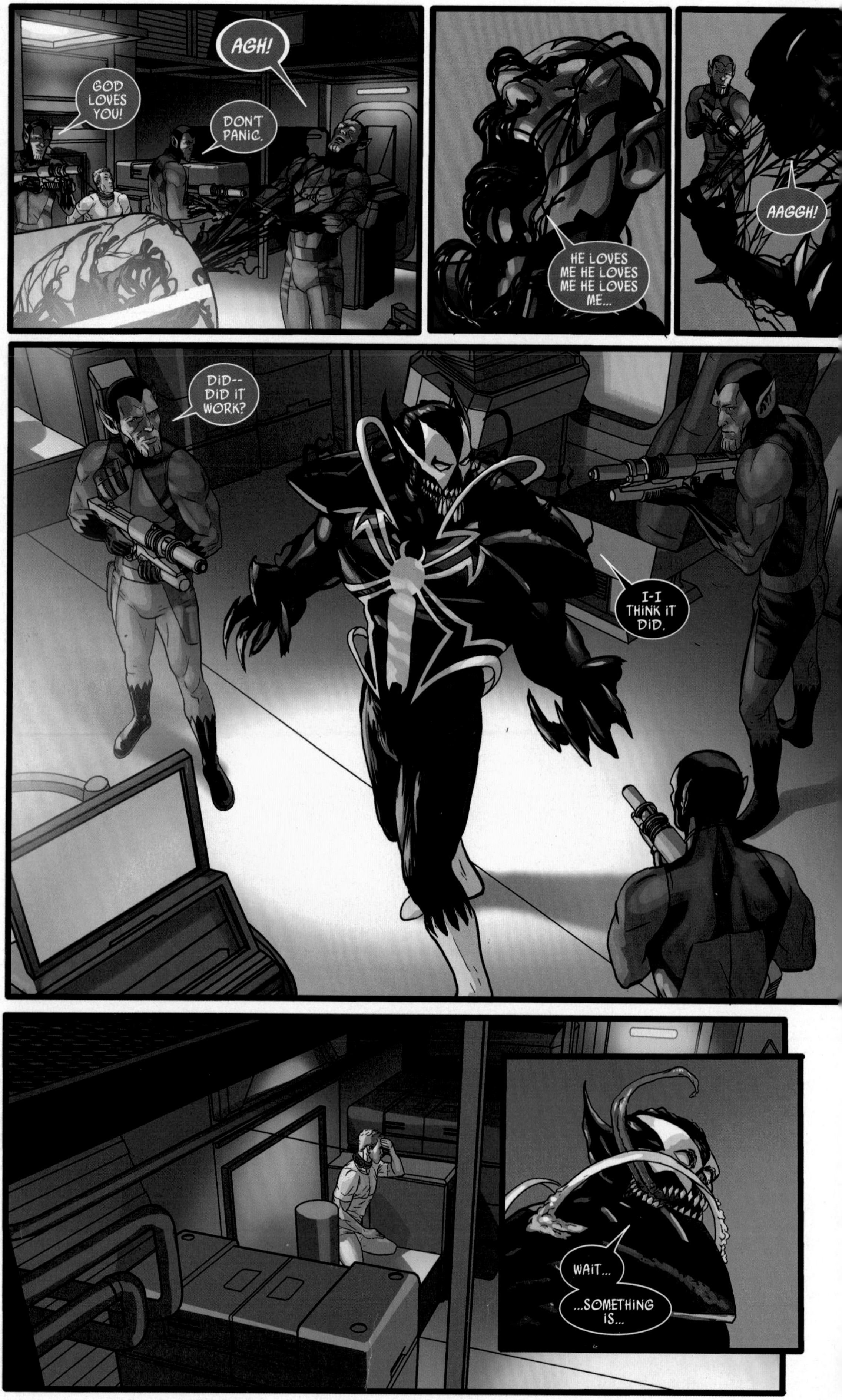
GOD LOVES YOU!
DON'T PANIC.
AGH!
HE LOVES ME HE LOVES ME HE LOVES ME...
AAGGH!
DID-- DID IT WORK?
I-I THINK IT DID.
WAIT...
...SOMETHING IS...

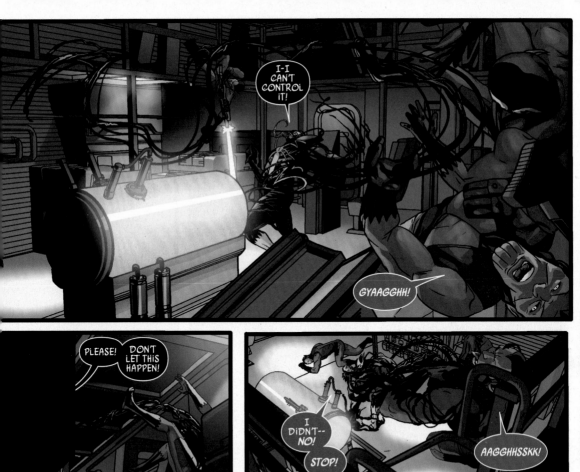

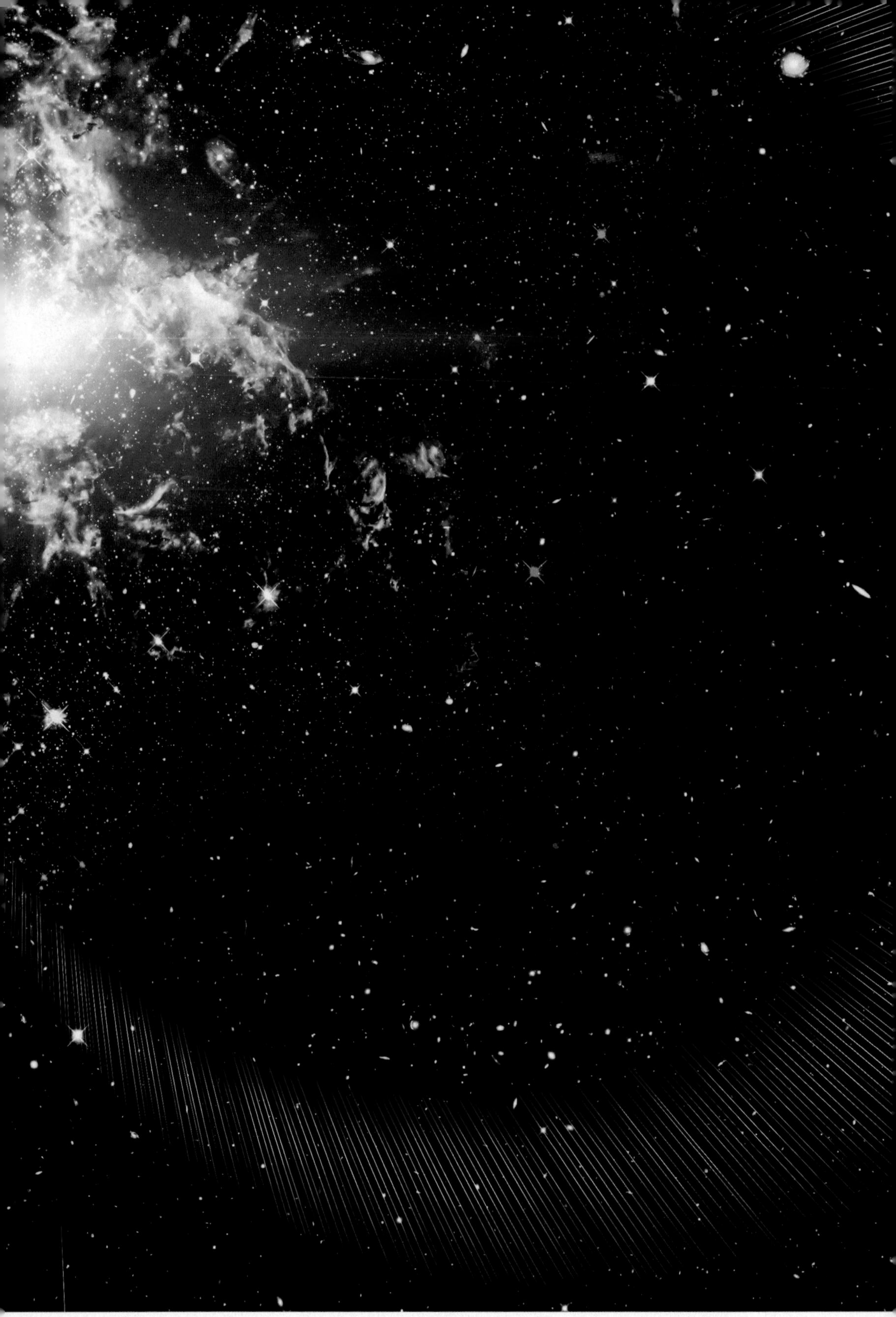

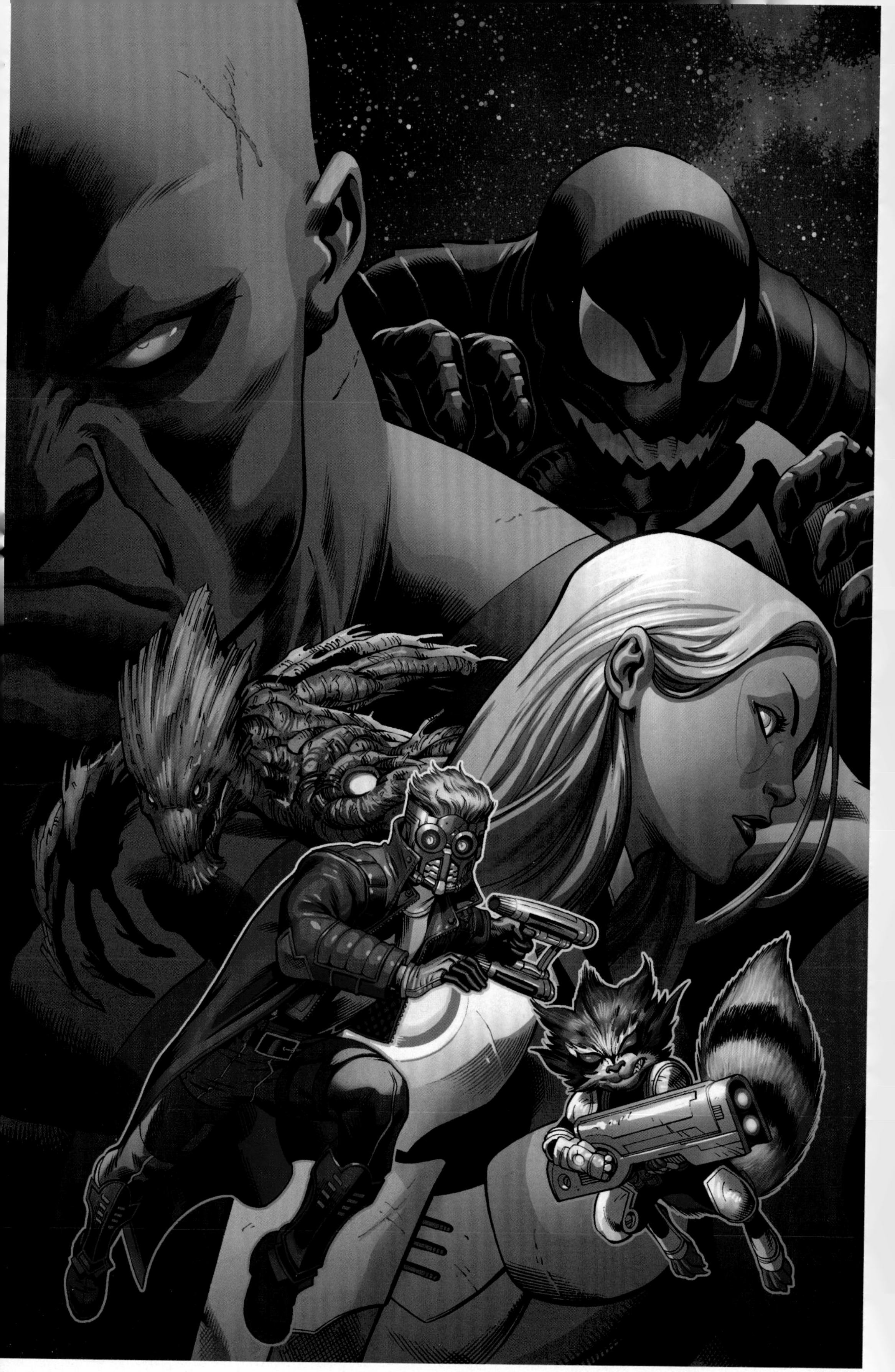

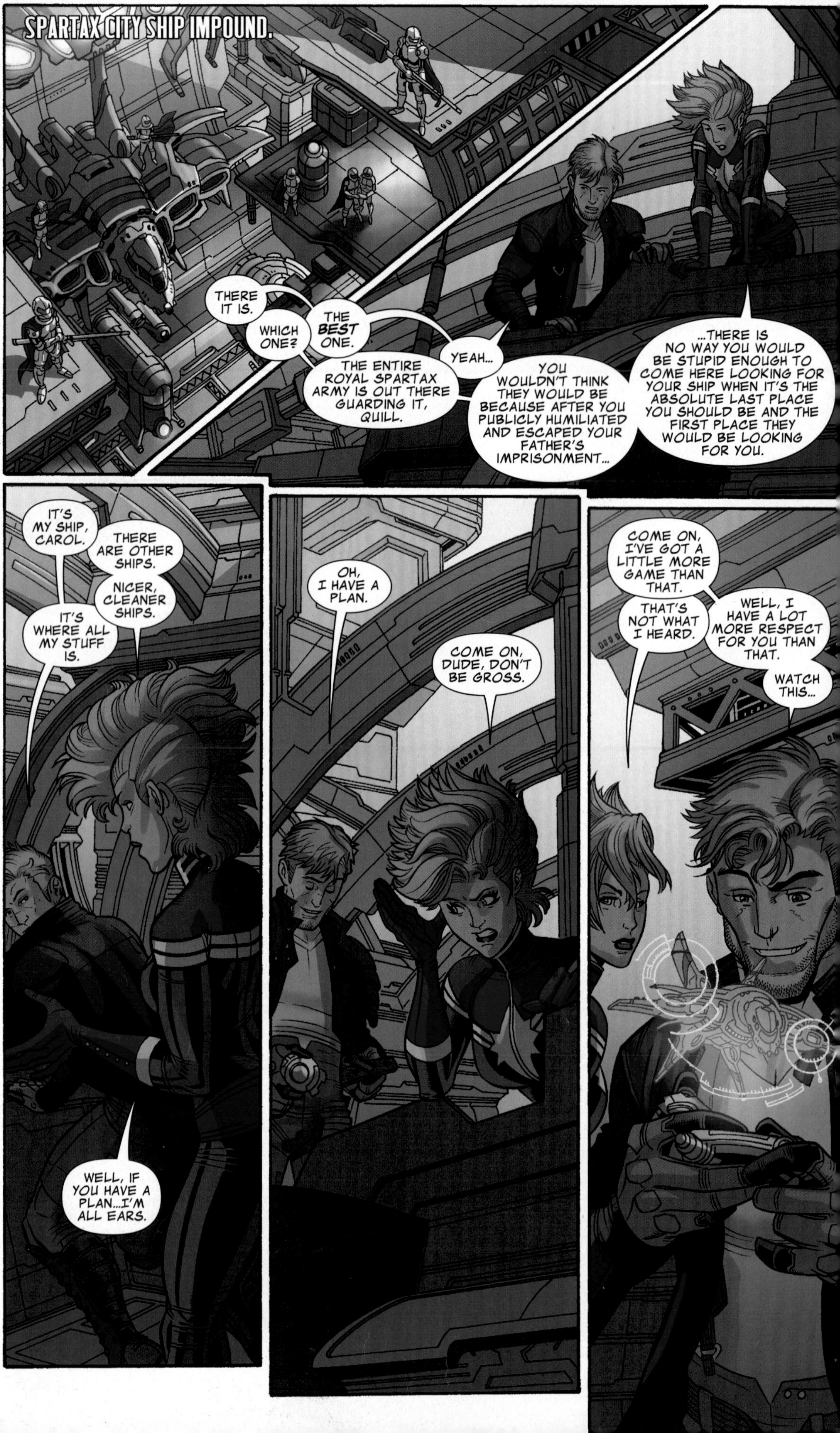
SPARTAX CITY SHIP IMPOUND.
THERE IT IS.
WHICH ONE?
THE BEST ONE.
YEAH...
THE ENTIRE ROYAL SPARTAX ARMY IS OUT THERE GUARDING IT, QUILL.
YOU WOULDN'T THINK THEY WOULD BE BECAUSE AFTER YOU PUBLICLY HUMILIATED AND ESCAPED YOUR FATHER'S IMPRISONMENT...
...THERE IS NO WAY YOU WOULD BE STUPID ENOUGH TO COME HERE LOOKING FOR YOUR SHIP WHEN IT'S THE ABSOLUTE LAST PLACE YOU SHOULD BE AND THE FIRST PLACE THEY WOULD BE LOOKING FOR YOU.
IT'S MY SHIP, CAROL.
THERE ARE OTHER SHIPS.
NICER, CLEANER SHIPS.
IT'S WHERE ALL MY STUFF IS.
WELL, IF YOU HAVE A PLAN...I'M ALL EARS.
OH, I HAVE A PLAN.
COME ON, DUDE, DON'T BE GROSS.
COME ON, I'VE GOT A LITTLE MORE GAME THAN THAT.
THAT'S NOT WHAT I HEARD.
WELL, I HAVE A LOT MORE RESPECT FOR YOU THAN THAT.
WATCH THIS...

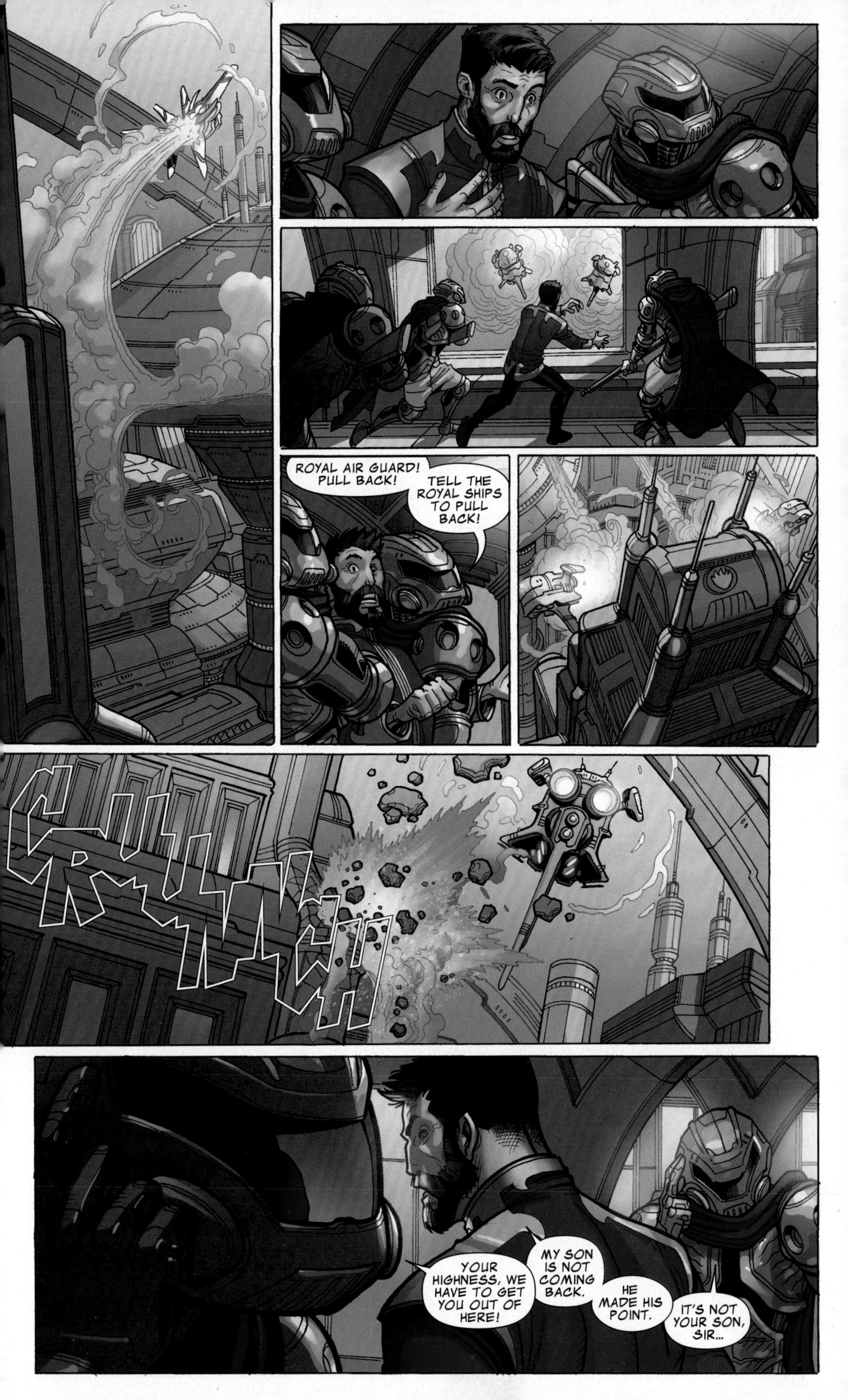
ROYAL AIR GUARD! PULL BACK!
TELL THE ROYAL SHIPS TO PULL BACK!
YOUR HIGHNESS, WE HAVE TO GET YOU OUT OF HERE!
MY SON IS NOT COMING BACK.
HE MADE HIS POINT.
IT'S NOT YOUR SON, SIR...

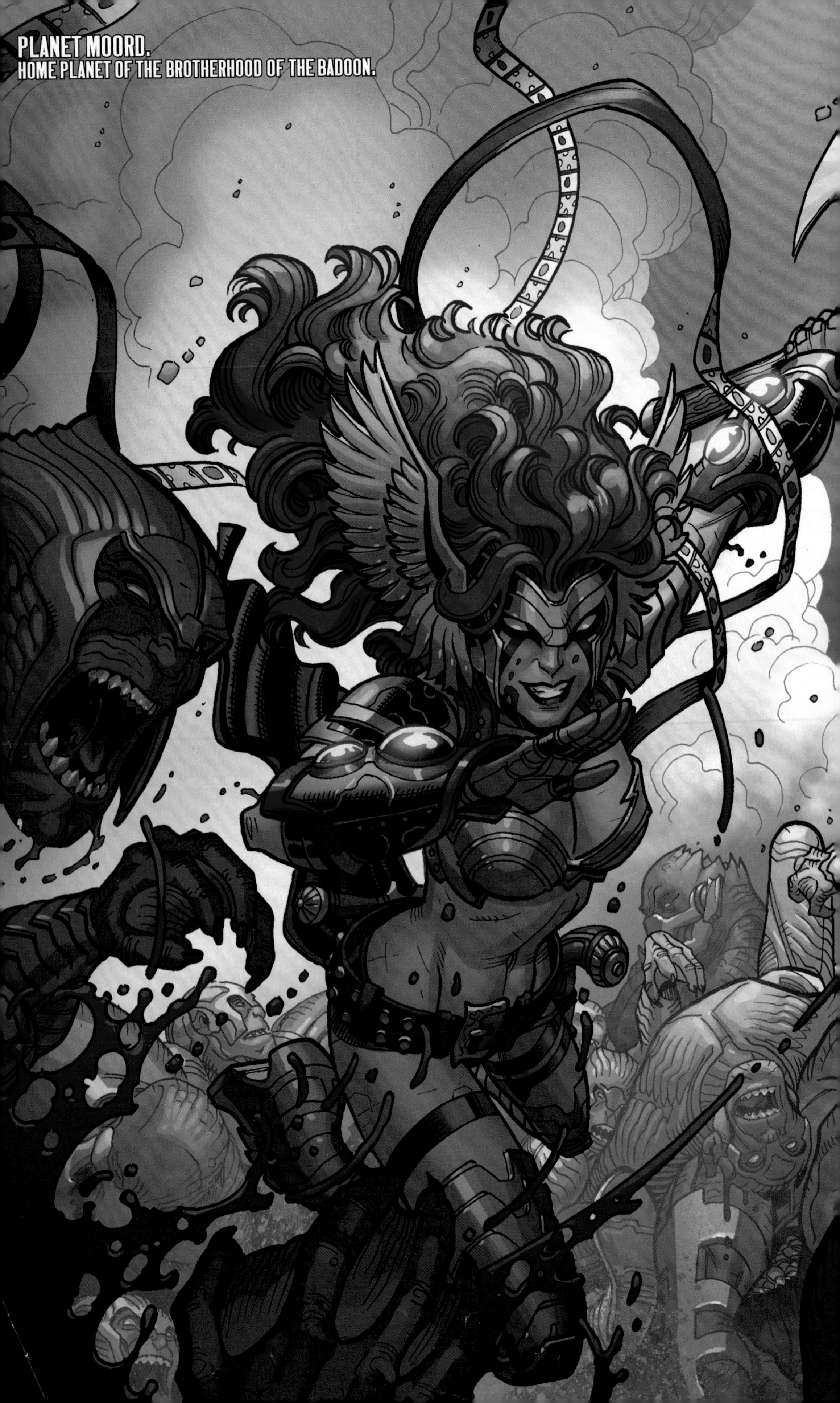
PLANET MOORD.
HOME PLANET OF THE BROTHERHOOD OF THE BADOON.

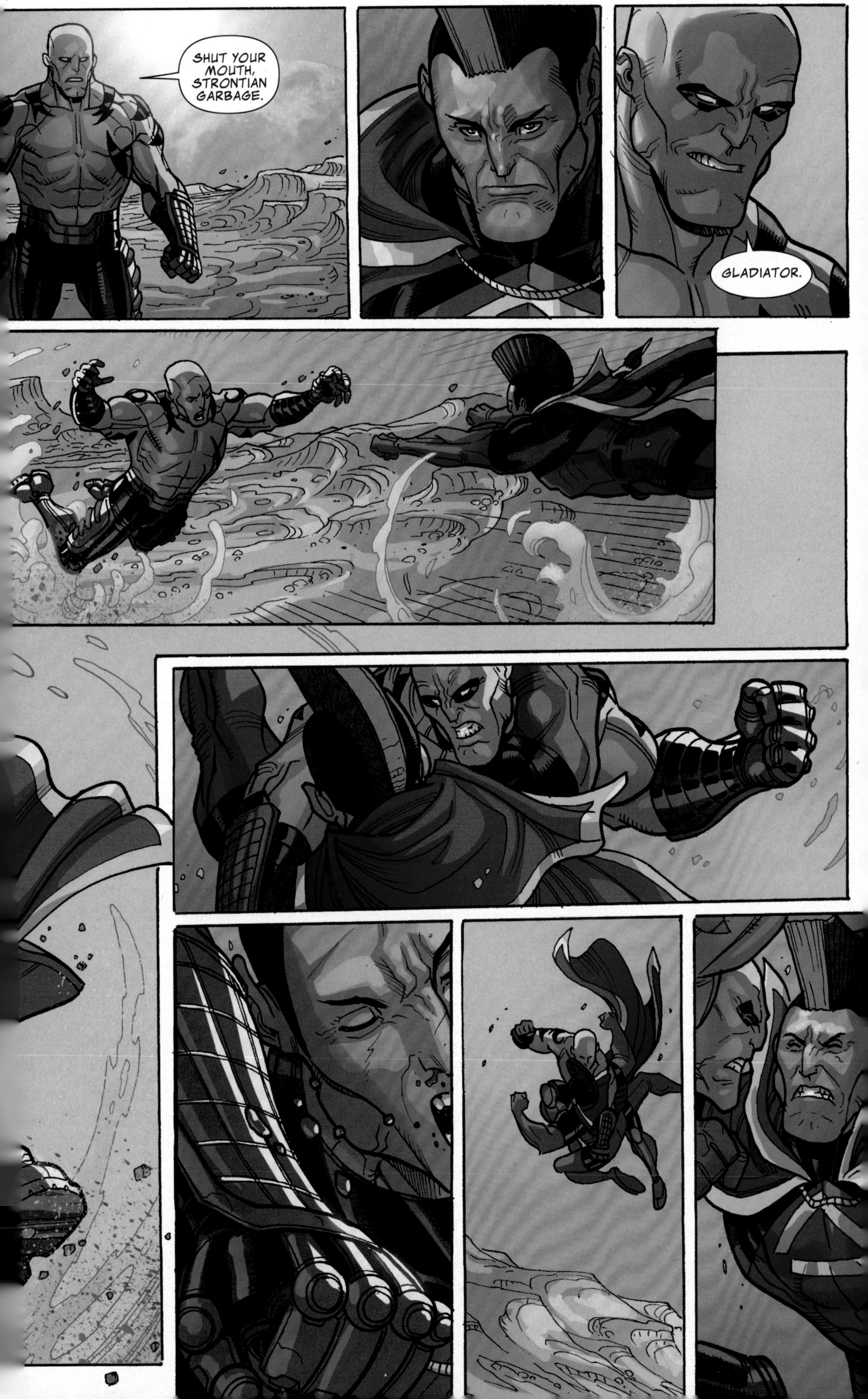
SHUT YOUR MOUTH, STRONTIAN GARBAGE.
GLADIATOR.

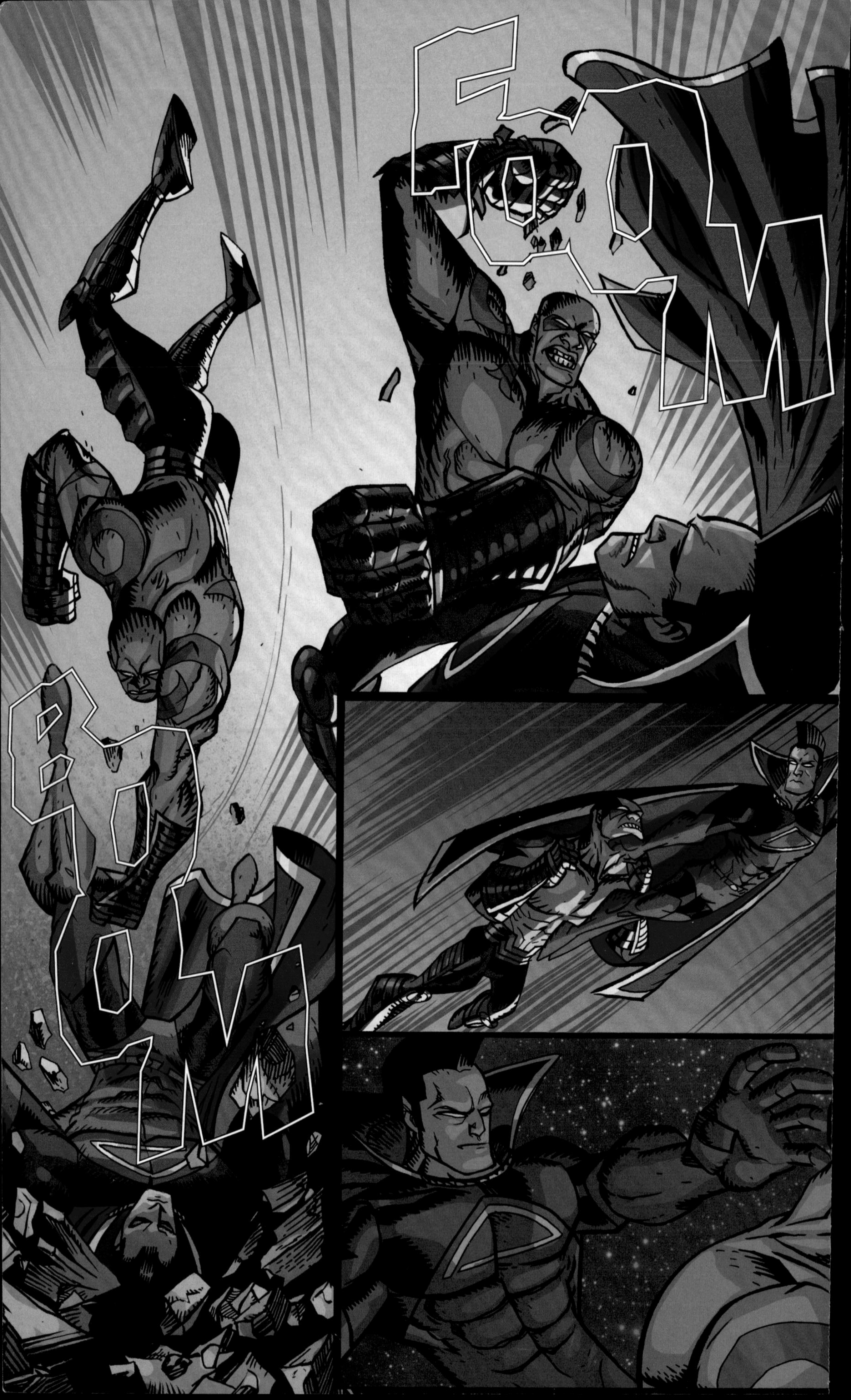
FOOM
BOOM

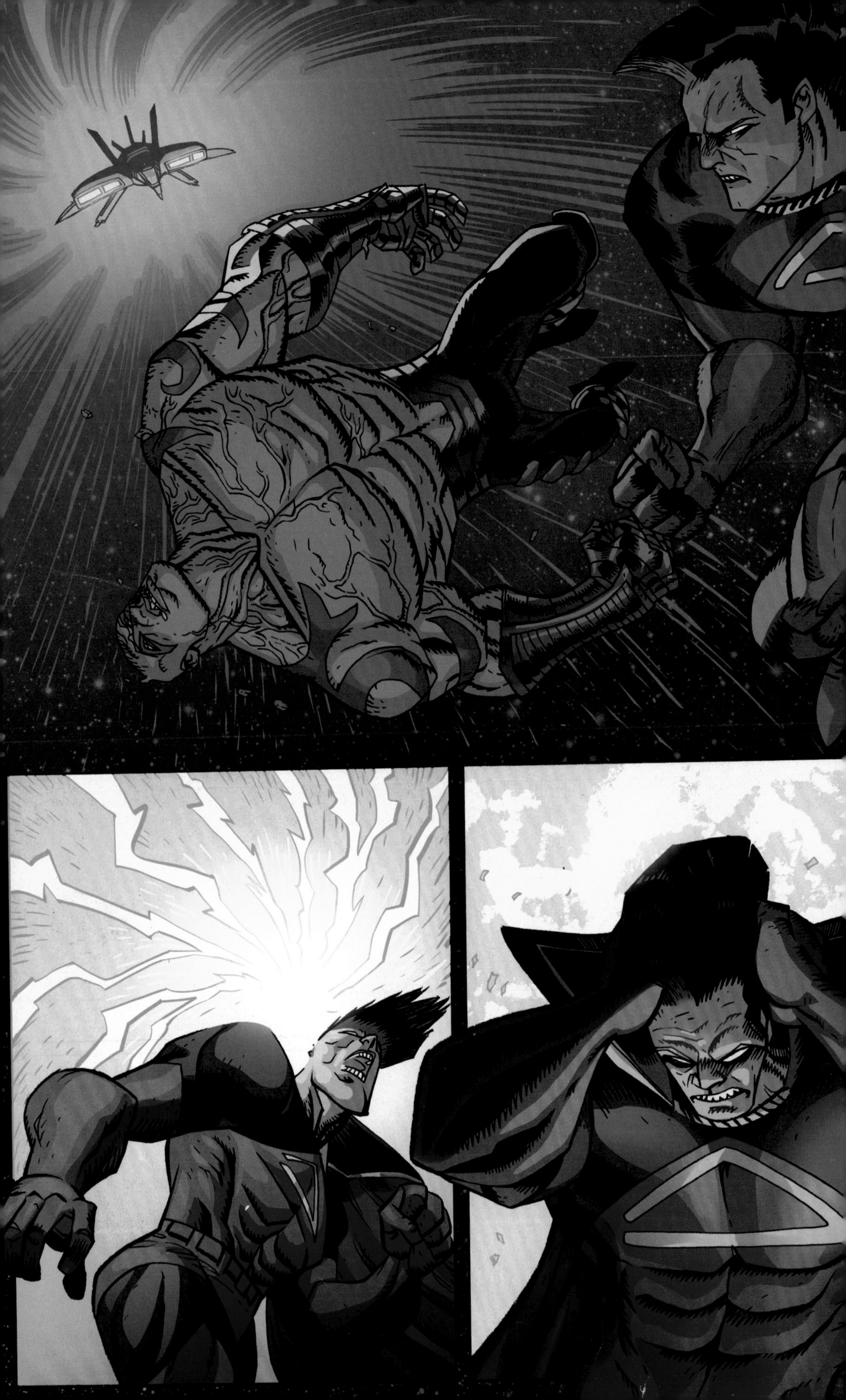

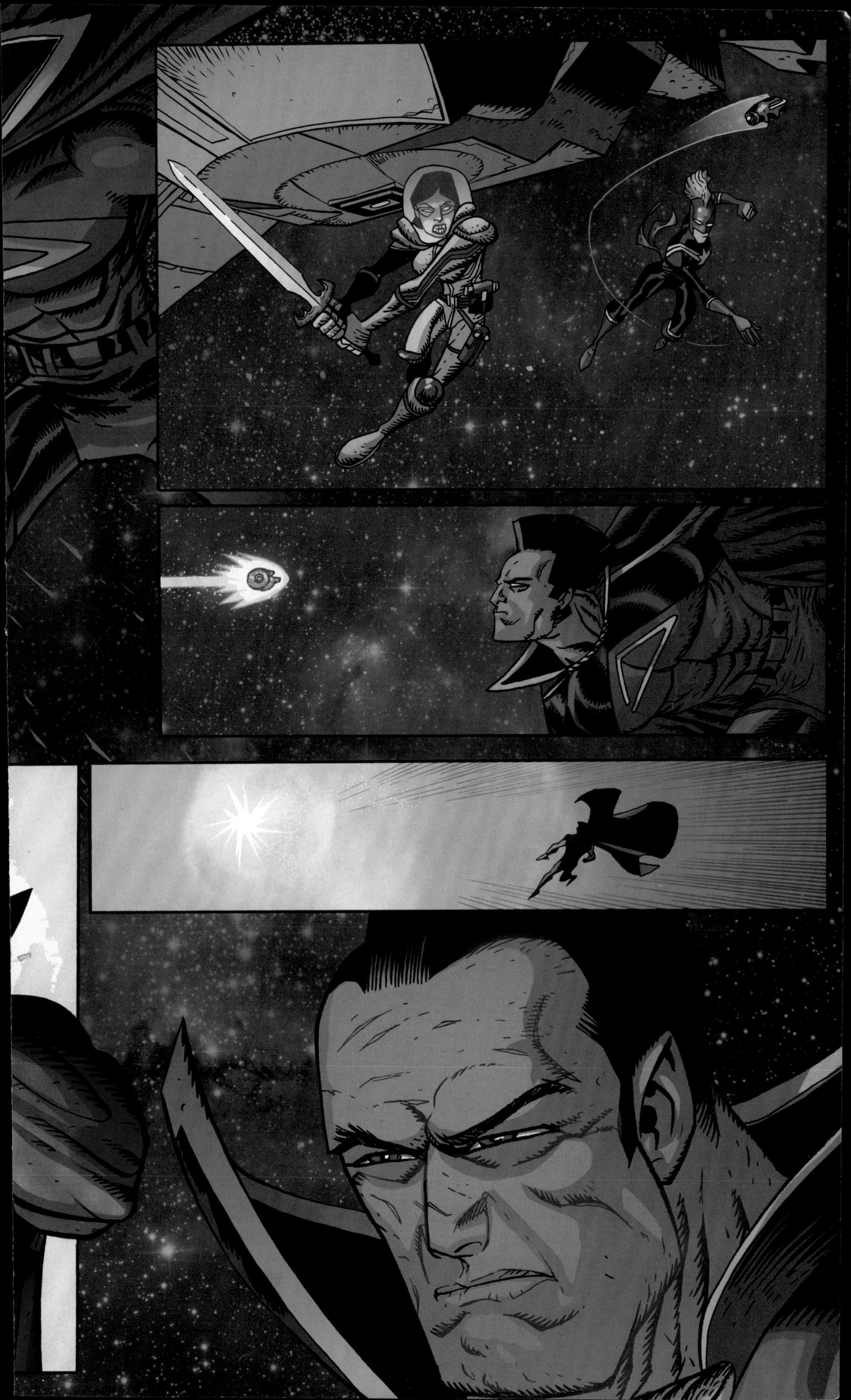

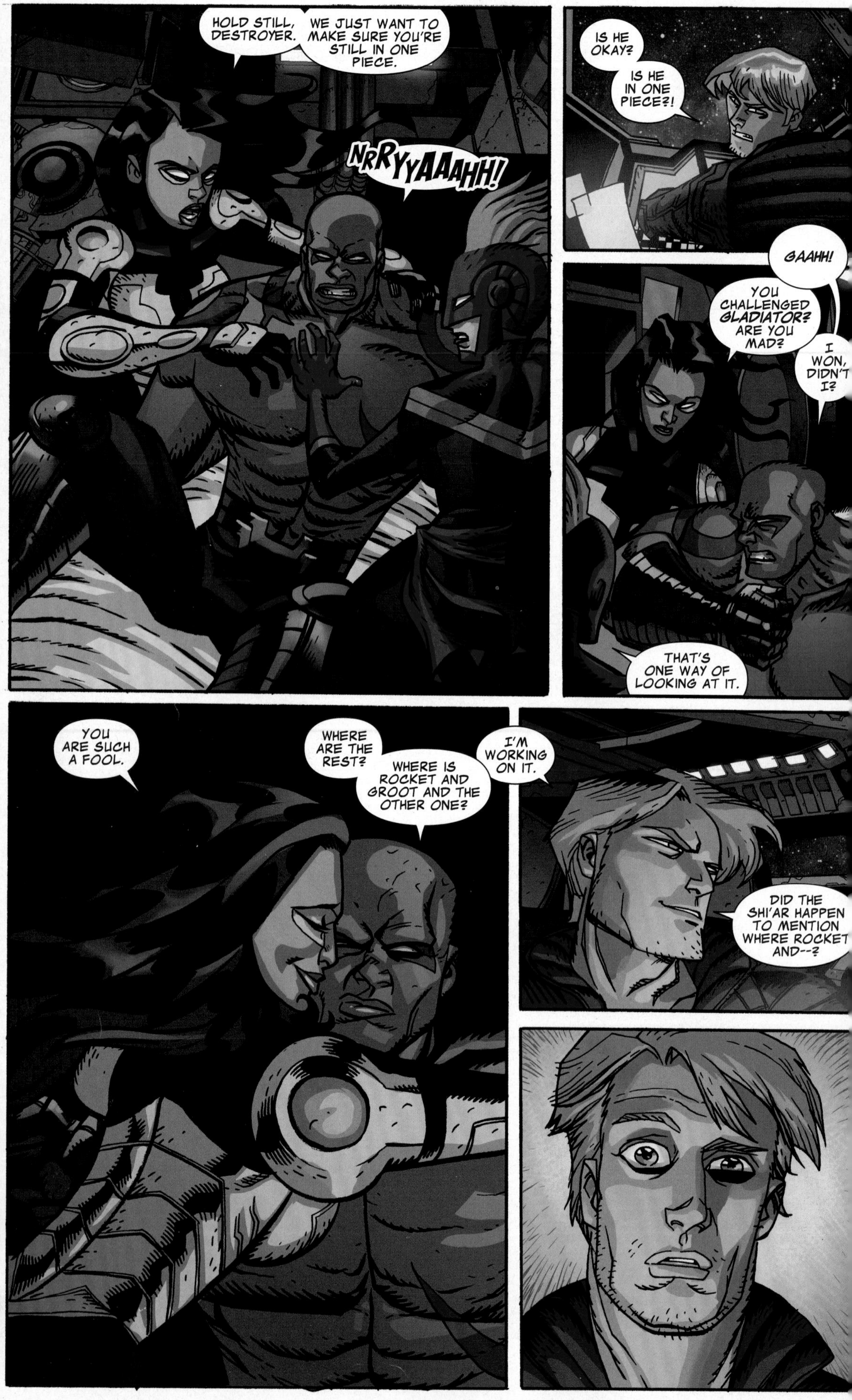
HOLD STILL, DESTROYER.
WE JUST WANT TO MAKE SURE YOU'RE STILL IN ONE PIECE.
NRRYYAAAHH!
IS HE OKAY?
IS HE IN ONE PIECE?!
GAAHH!
YOU CHALLENGED GLADIATOR? ARE YOU MAD?
I WON, DIDN'T I?
THAT'S ONE WAY OF LOOKING AT IT.
YOU ARE SUCH A FOOL.
WHERE ARE THE REST?
WHERE IS ROCKET AND GROOT AND THE OTHER ONE?
I'M WORKING ON IT.
DID THE SHI'AR HAPPEN TO MENTION WHERE ROCKET AND--?

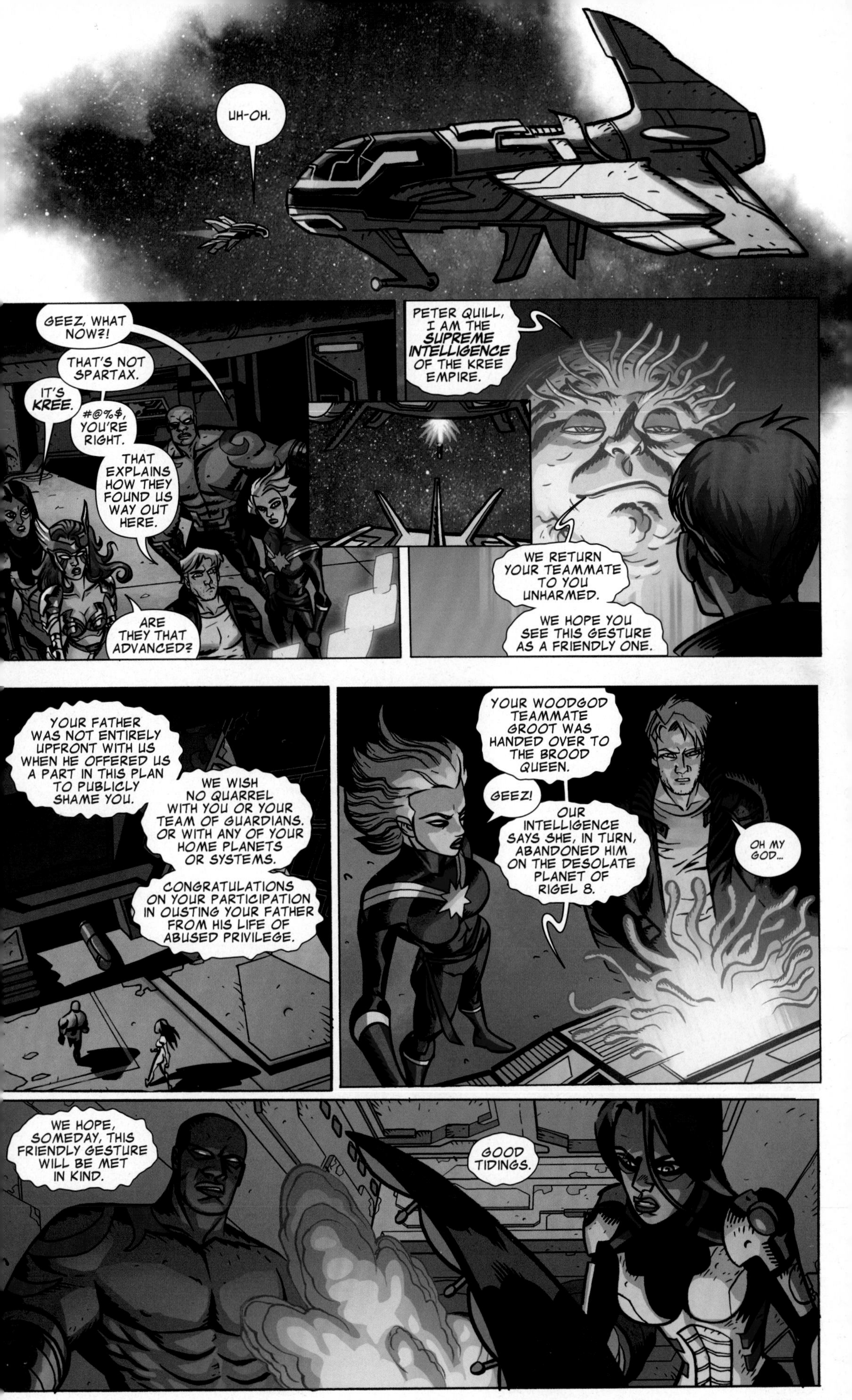
UH-OH.
GEEZ, WHAT NOW?!
THAT'S NOT SPARTAX.
IT'S KREE.
#@%$, YOU'RE RIGHT.
THAT EXPLAINS HOW THEY FOUND US WAY OUT HERE.
ARE THEY THAT ADVANCED?
PETER QUILL, I AM THE SUPREME INTELLIGENCE OF THE KREE EMPIRE.
WE RETURN YOUR TEAMMATE TO YOU UNHARMED.
WE HOPE YOU SEE THIS GESTURE AS A FRIENDLY ONE.
YOUR FATHER WAS NOT ENTIRELY UPFRONT WITH US WHEN HE OFFERED US A PART IN THIS PLAN TO PUBLICLY SHAME YOU.
WE WISH NO QUARREL WITH YOU OR YOUR TEAM OF GUARDIANS. OR WITH ANY OF YOUR HOME PLANETS OR SYSTEMS.
CONGRATULATIONS ON YOUR PARTICIPATION IN OUSTING YOUR FATHER FROM HIS LIFE OF ABUSED PRIVILEGE.
YOUR WOODGOD TEAMMATE GROOT WAS HANDED OVER TO THE BROOD QUEEN.
GEEZ!
OUR INTELLIGENCE SAYS SHE, IN TURN, ABANDONED HIM ON THE DESOLATE PLANET OF RIGEL 8.
OH MY GOD...
WE HOPE, SOMEDAY, THIS FRIENDLY GESTURE WILL BE MET IN KIND.
GOOD TIDINGS.

NEXT: THE TRUTH ABOUT
RICHARD RYDER, THE CANCERVERSE, AND THANOS.

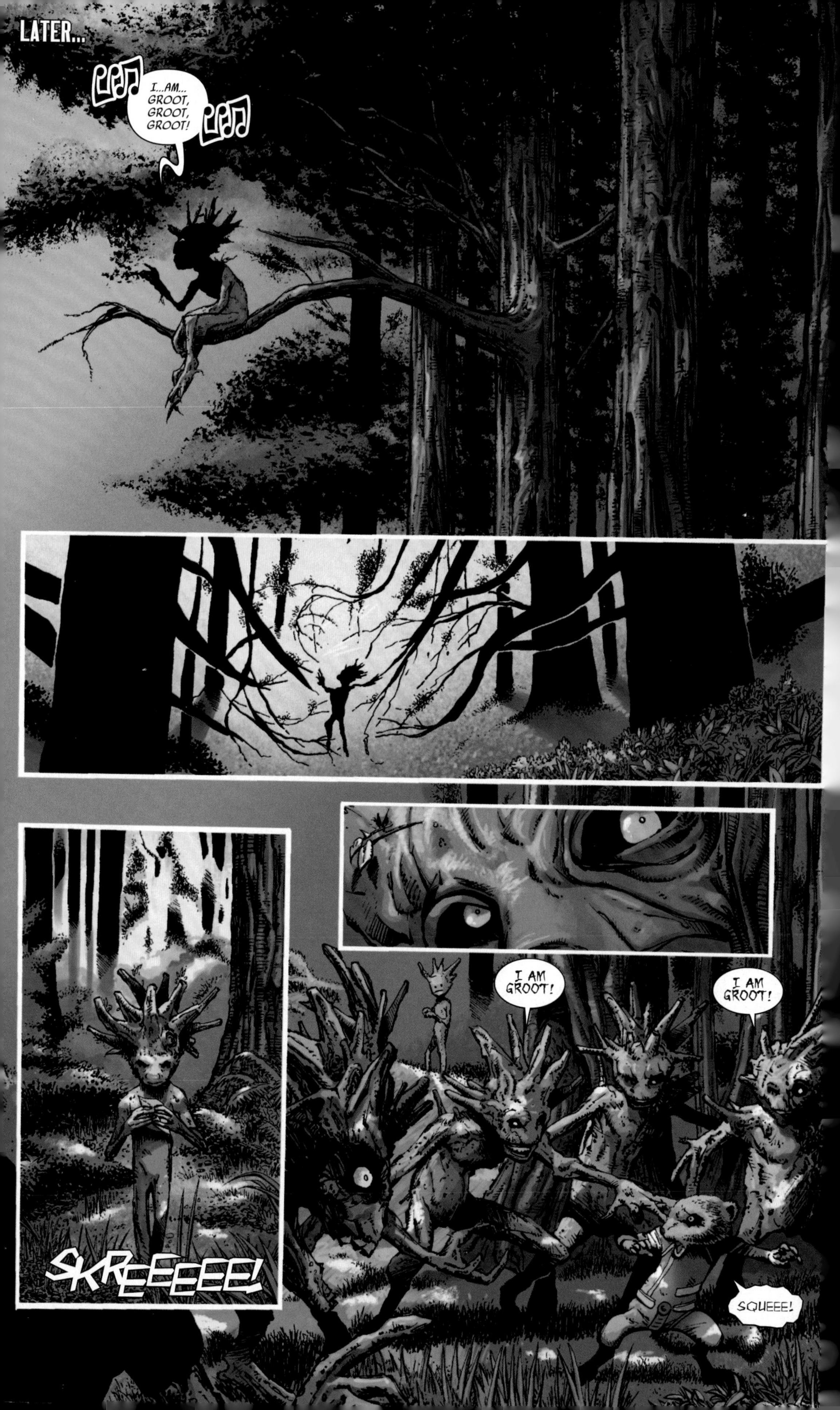
LATER...
I...AM... GROOT, GROOT, GROOT!
I AM GROOT!
I AM GROOT!
SKREEEEEE!
SQUEEE!

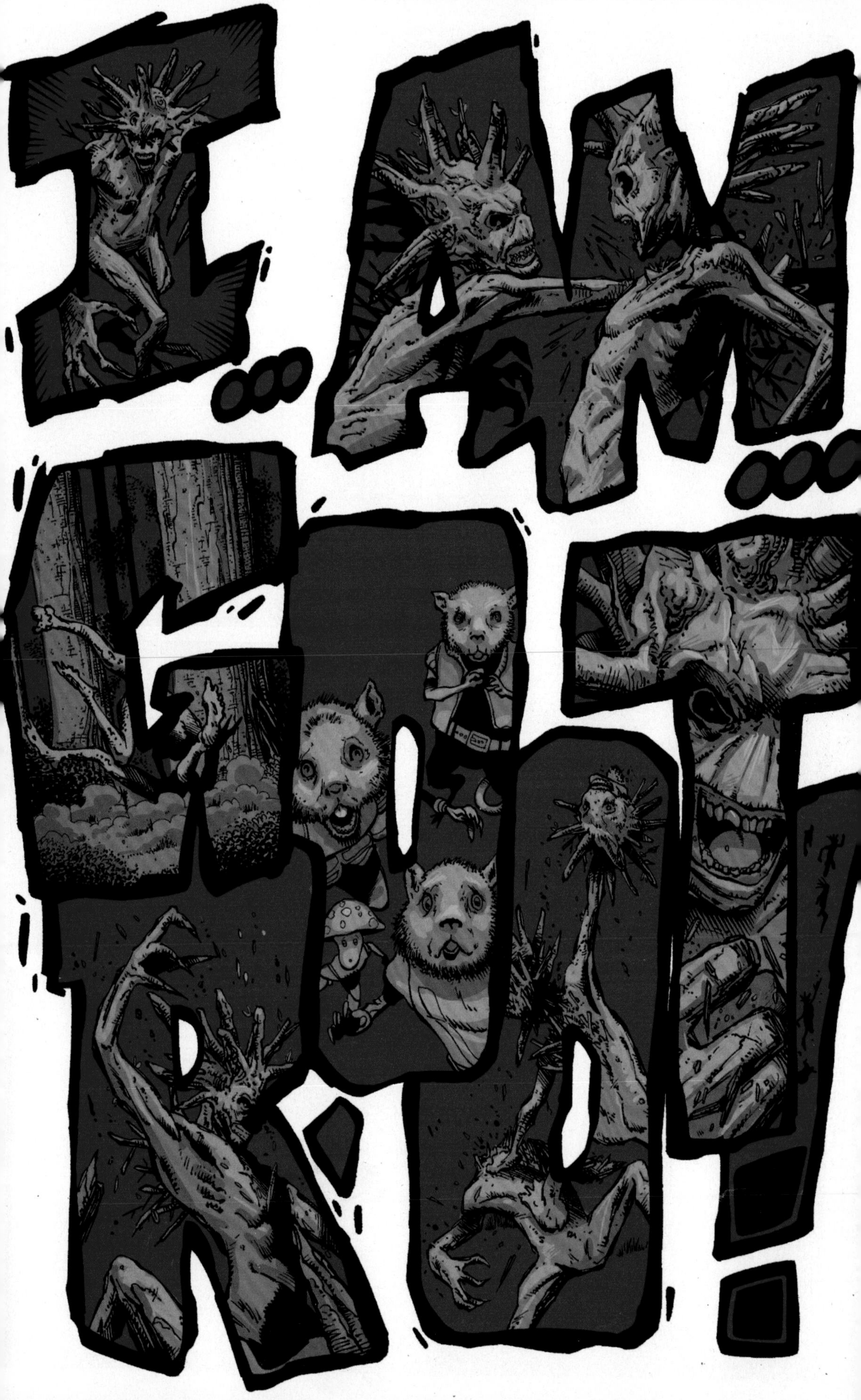
I... AM... GROOT!

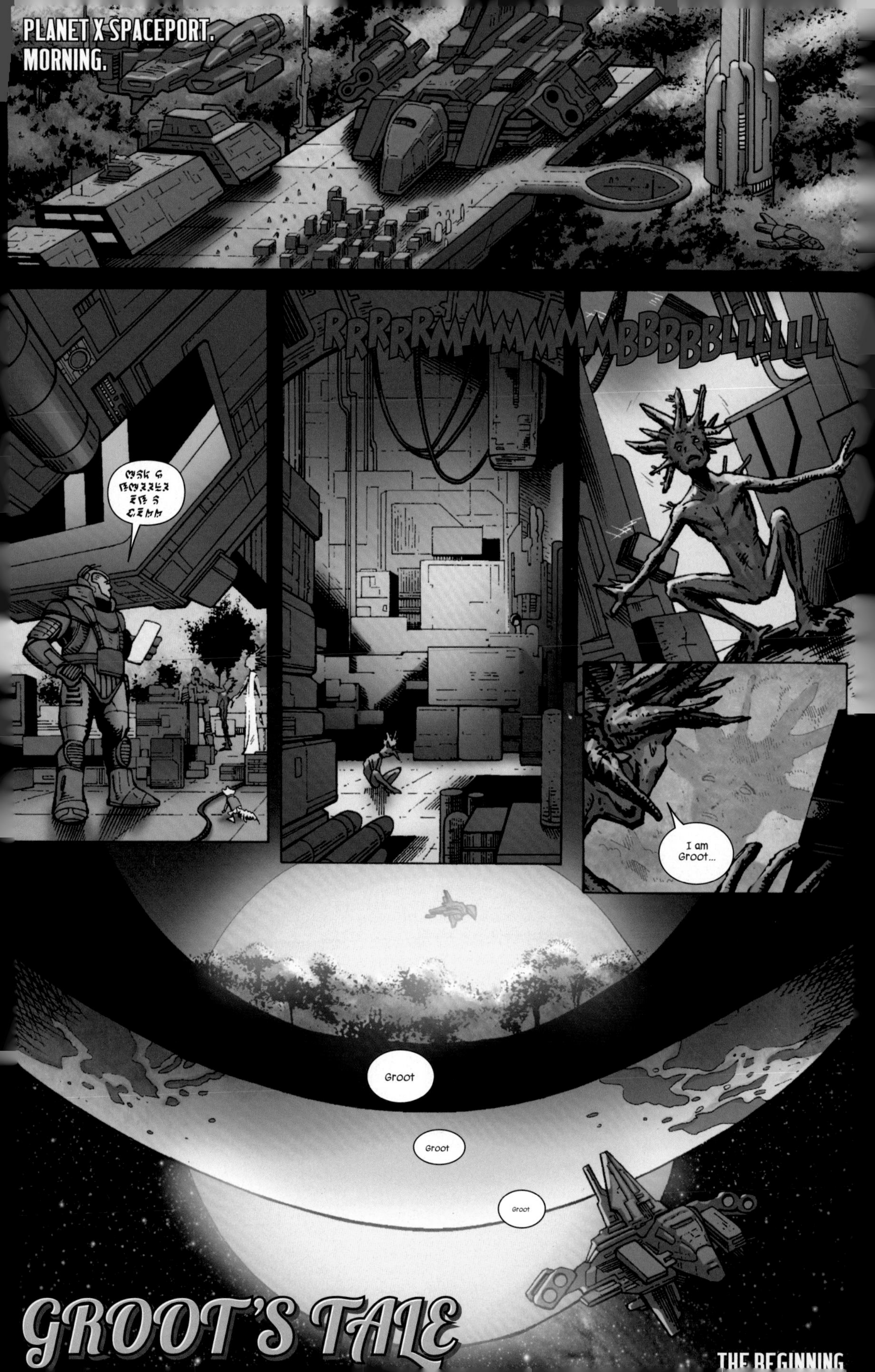
PLANET X SPACEPORT.
MORNING.
RRRRRMMMMMMMMBBBBBLLLLLLL
I am Groot...
Groot
Groot
Groot
GROOT'S TALE
THE BEGINNING

EARTH, 3014 A.D.

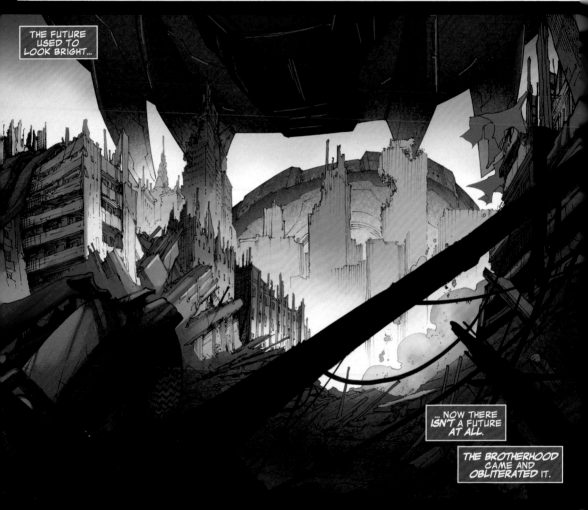

THE FUTURE USED TO LOOK BRIGHT...

... NOW THERE ISN'T A FUTURE AT ALL.

THE BROTHERHOOD CAME AND OBLITERATED IT.

EARTH *BURNED.* SO DID THE *OTHER* PEACEFUL WORLDS OF THE UNITED SYSTEM.

HUMAN CULTURE COLLAPSED *OVERNIGHT.*

MY NAME IS *GEENA DRAKE.* I WILL BE DEAD IN *THREE DAYS.*

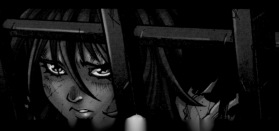

I ARRIVED AT LABOR CAMP 347 LAST NIGHT. THEY TELL ME *THREE DAYS* IS THE TYPICAL LIFE EXPECTANCY FOR A SLAVE WORKER.

THE STORIES CALL HIM VANCE ASTRO.

THEY SAY HE IS A *THOUSAND* YEARS OLD, A MAN FROM ANOTHER AGE BROUGHT TO *OURS* BY SOME ACCIDENT OF CRYOGENIC SUSPENSION.

WHAT HIS BLOWS DO NOT FELL--

HE IS *NOT* A MAN.

HE IS A *BLUR*.

HE MOVES WITH *IMPOSSIBLE* AGILITY, HIS MOVEMENTS BOOSTED AND ENHANCED BY PSIONIC IMPULSES.

--HIS MIND *LEVELS*.

HE CARRIES THE SHIELD OF AN *ANCIENT HERO*. IT REPRESENTS AN *IDEAL*.

IT IS A SYMBOL OF *LIBERTY* AND *EQUALITY* FOR THE *ENTIRE* UNITED SYSTEM.

GUARDIANS!

AGAIN, THE PSIONIC CALL.

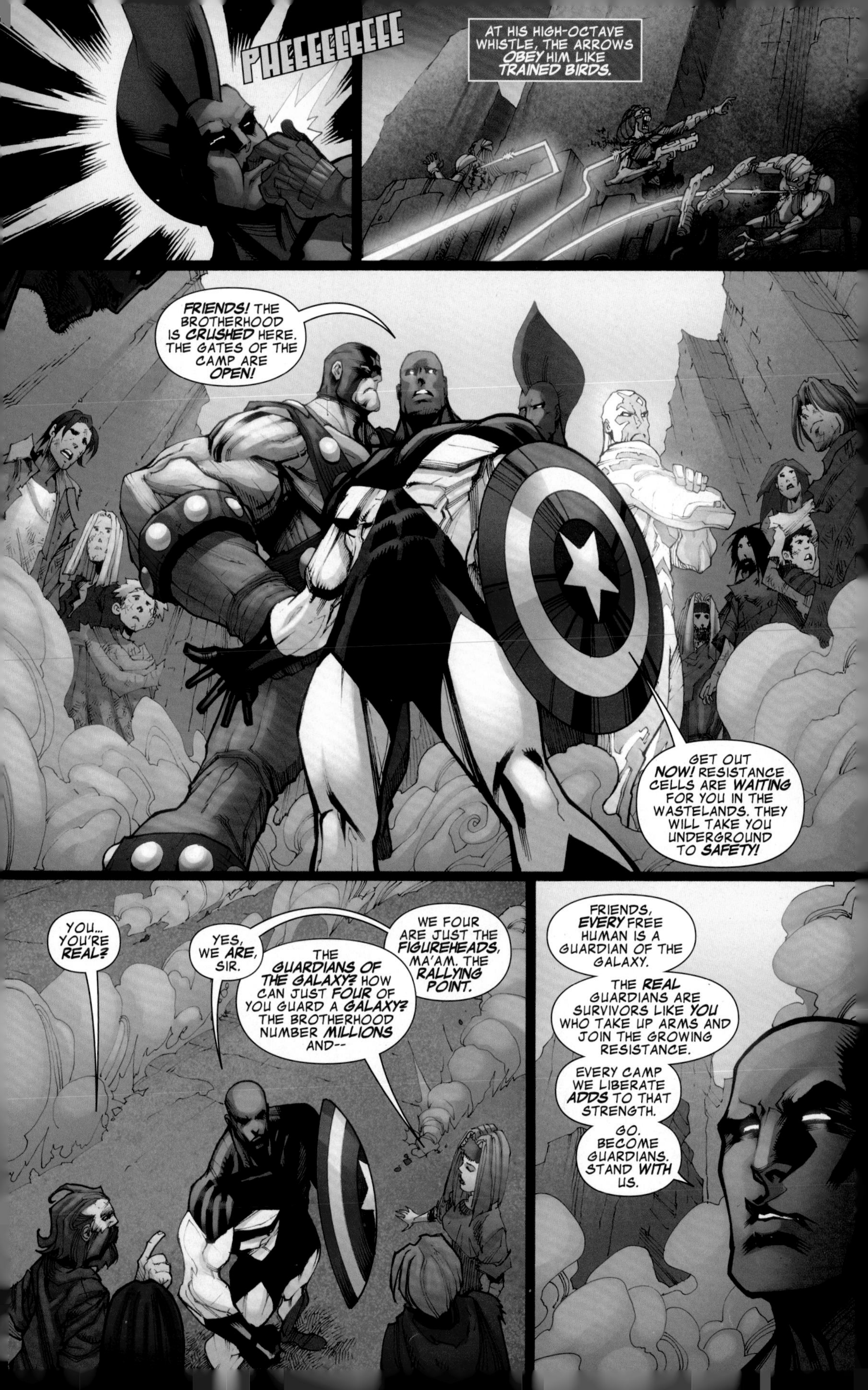
PHEEEEEEEEEE
AT HIS HIGH-OCTAVE WHISTLE, THE ARROWS OBEY HIM LIKE TRAINED BIRDS.
FRIENDS! THE BROTHERHOOD IS CRUSHED HERE. THE GATES OF THE CAMP ARE OPEN!
GET OUT NOW! RESISTANCE CELLS ARE WAITING FOR YOU IN THE WASTELANDS. THEY WILL TAKE YOU UNDERGROUND TO SAFETY!
YOU... YOU'RE REAL?
YES, WE ARE, SIR.
THE GUARDIANS OF THE GALAXY? HOW CAN JUST FOUR OF YOU GUARD A GALAXY? THE BROTHERHOOD NUMBER MILLIONS AND--
WE FOUR ARE JUST THE FIGUREHEADS, MA'AM. THE RALLYING POINT.
FRIENDS, EVERY FREE HUMAN IS A GUARDIAN OF THE GALAXY.
THE REAL GUARDIANS ARE SURVIVORS LIKE YOU WHO TAKE UP ARMS AND JOIN THE GROWING RESISTANCE.
EVERY CAMP WE LIBERATE ADDS TO THAT STRENGTH.
GO. BECOME GUARDIANS. STAND WITH US.

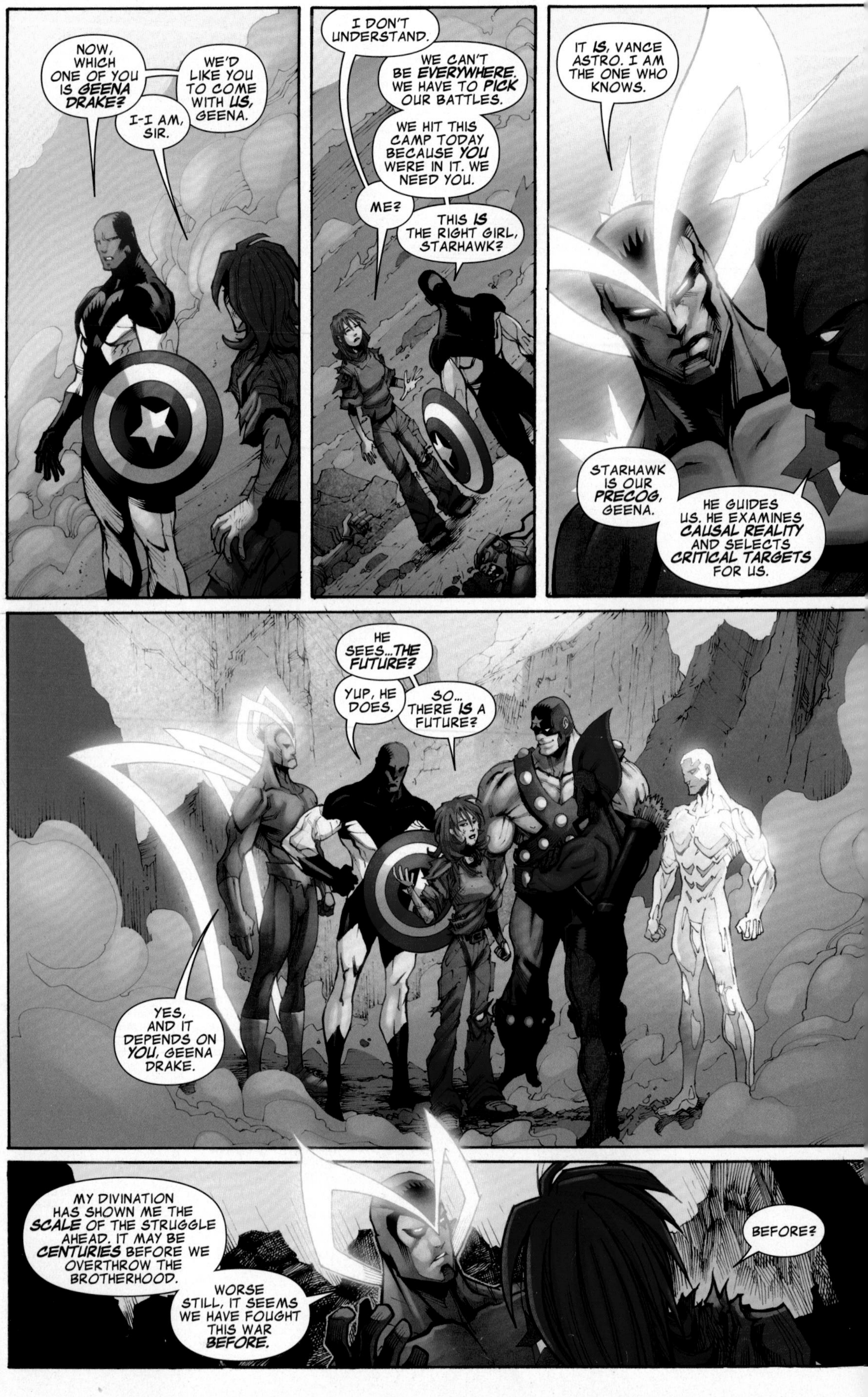
NOW, WHICH ONE OF YOU IS GEENA DRAKE?
WE'D LIKE YOU TO COME WITH US, GEENA.
I-I AM, SIR.
I DON'T UNDERSTAND.
WE CAN'T BE EVERYWHERE. WE HAVE TO PICK OUR BATTLES.
WE HIT THIS CAMP TODAY BECAUSE YOU WERE IN IT. WE NEED YOU.
ME?
THIS IS THE RIGHT GIRL, STARHAWK?
IT IS, VANCE ASTRO. I AM THE ONE WHO KNOWS.
STARHAWK IS OUR PRECOG, GEENA.
HE GUIDES US. HE EXAMINES CAUSAL REALITY AND SELECTS CRITICAL TARGETS FOR US.
HE SEES...THE FUTURE?
YUP, HE DOES.
SO... THERE IS A FUTURE?
YES, AND IT DEPENDS ON YOU, GEENA DRAKE.
MY DIVINATION HAS SHOWN ME THE SCALE OF THE STRUGGLE AHEAD. IT MAY BE CENTURIES BEFORE WE OVERTHROW THE BROTHERHOOD.
WORSE STILL, IT SEEMS WE HAVE FOUGHT THIS WAR BEFORE.
BEFORE?

THWWSHHHHHHHHH

THREE SECONDS IN A MUSEUM AND YOU'RE SOUND ASLEEP.

WHY AM I NOT SURPRISED?

KCK

KCK

NEXT TIME I'LL SKIP THE PUNCHING AND JUST READ YOU A BOOK.

...AND WHAT CAN YOU TELL US ABOUT YOUR NEW ALLY?

WHAT NEW--? OH.

WHAT...?

YOU KNOW WHAT.

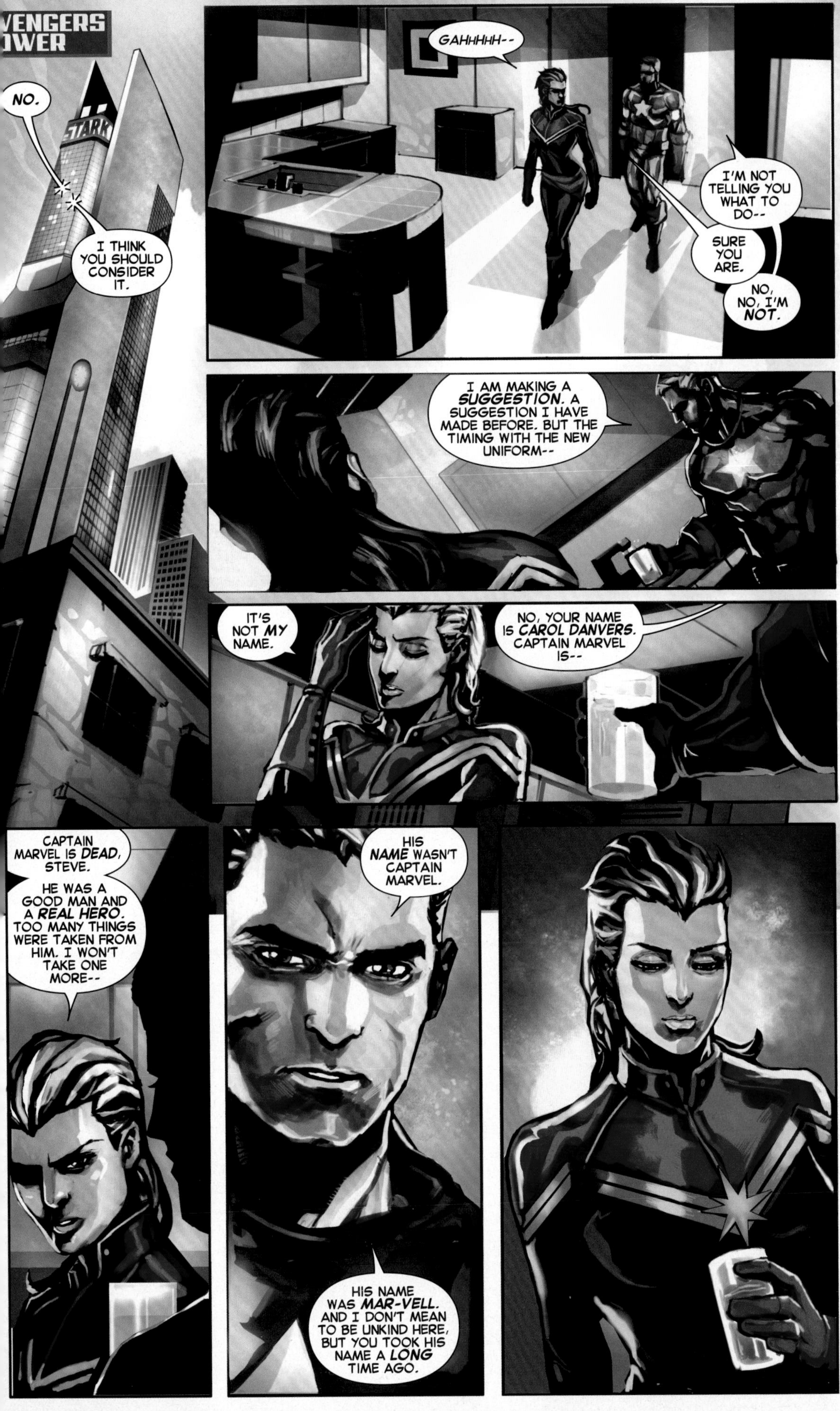

VENGERS
OWER
NO.
I THINK YOU SHOULD CONSIDER IT.
STARK
GAHHHHH--
I'M NOT TELLING YOU WHAT TO DO--
SURE YOU ARE.
NO, NO, I'M NOT.
I AM MAKING A SUGGESTION. A SUGGESTION I HAVE MADE BEFORE. BUT THE TIMING WITH THE NEW UNIFORM--
IT'S NOT MY NAME.
NO, YOUR NAME IS CAROL DANVERS. CAPTAIN MARVEL IS--
CAPTAIN MARVEL IS DEAD, STEVE.
HE WAS A GOOD MAN AND A REAL HERO. TOO MANY THINGS WERE TAKEN FROM HIM. I WON'T TAKE ONE MORE--
HIS NAME WASN'T CAPTAIN MARVEL.
HIS NAME WAS MAR-VELL. AND I DON'T MEAN TO BE UNKIND HERE, BUT YOU TOOK HIS NAME A LONG TIME AGO.

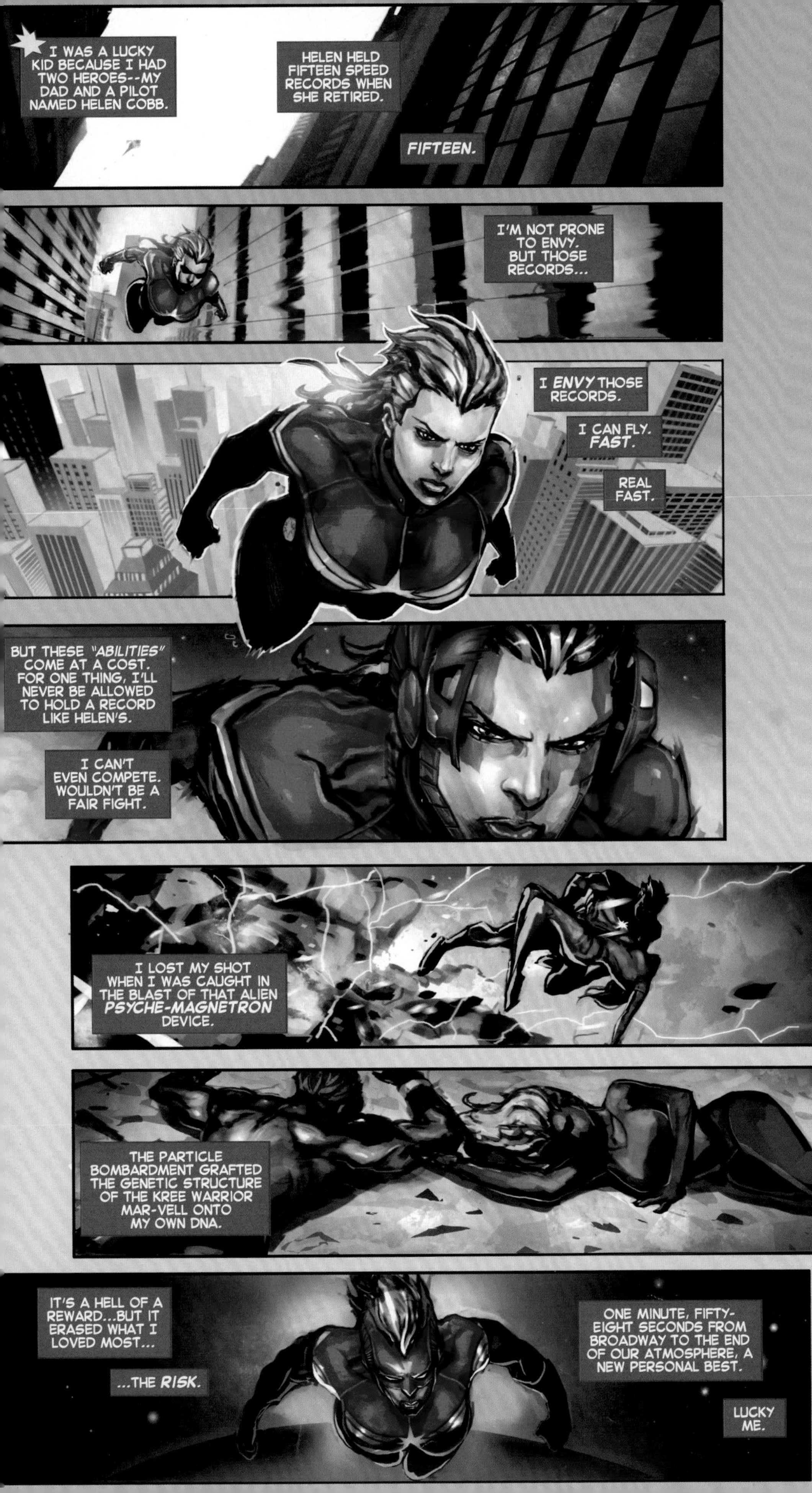
I WAS A LUCKY KID BECAUSE I HAD TWO HEROES--MY DAD AND A PILOT NAMED HELEN COBB.
HELEN HELD FIFTEEN SPEED RECORDS WHEN SHE RETIRED.
FIFTEEN.
I'M NOT PRONE TO ENVY. BUT THOSE RECORDS...
I ENVY THOSE RECORDS.
I CAN FLY. FAST.
REAL FAST.
BUT THESE "ABILITIES" COME AT A COST. FOR ONE THING, I'LL NEVER BE ALLOWED TO HOLD A RECORD LIKE HELEN'S.
I CAN'T EVEN COMPETE. WOULDN'T BE A FAIR FIGHT.
I LOST MY SHOT WHEN I WAS CAUGHT IN THE BLAST OF THAT ALIEN PSYCHE-MAGNETRON DEVICE.
THE PARTICLE BOMBARDMENT GRAFTED THE GENETIC STRUCTURE OF THE KREE WARRIOR MAR-VELL ONTO MY OWN DNA.
IT'S A HELL OF A REWARD...BUT IT ERASED WHAT I LOVED MOST...
...THE RISK.
ONE MINUTE, FIFTY-EIGHT SECONDS FROM BROADWAY TO THE END OF OUR ATMOSPHERE, A NEW PERSONAL BEST.
LUCKY ME.

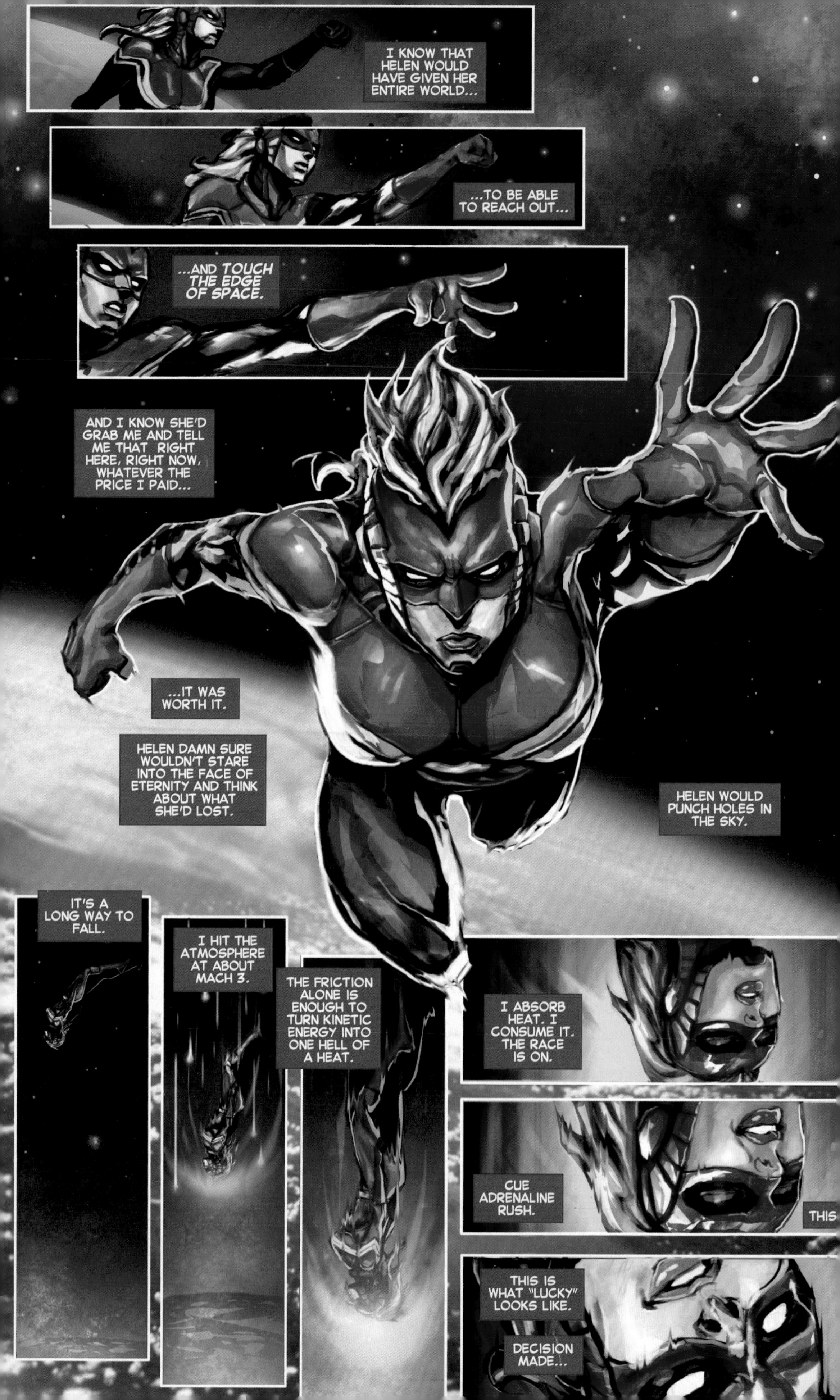
I KNOW THAT HELEN WOULD HAVE GIVEN HER ENTIRE WORLD...
...TO BE ABLE TO REACH OUT...
...AND TOUCH THE EDGE OF SPACE.
AND I KNOW SHE'D GRAB ME AND TELL ME THAT RIGHT HERE, RIGHT NOW, WHATEVER THE PRICE I PAID...
...IT WAS WORTH IT.
HELEN DAMN SURE WOULDN'T STARE INTO THE FACE OF ETERNITY AND THINK ABOUT WHAT SHE'D LOST.
HELEN WOULD PUNCH HOLES IN THE SKY.
IT'S A LONG WAY TO FALL.
I HIT THE ATMOSPHERE AT ABOUT MACH 3.
THE FRICTION ALONE IS ENOUGH TO TURN KINETIC ENERGY INTO ONE HELL OF A HEAT.
I ABSORB HEAT. I CONSUME IT. THE RACE IS ON.
CUE ADRENALINE RUSH.
THIS
THIS IS WHAT "LUCKY" LOOKS LIKE.
DECISION MADE...

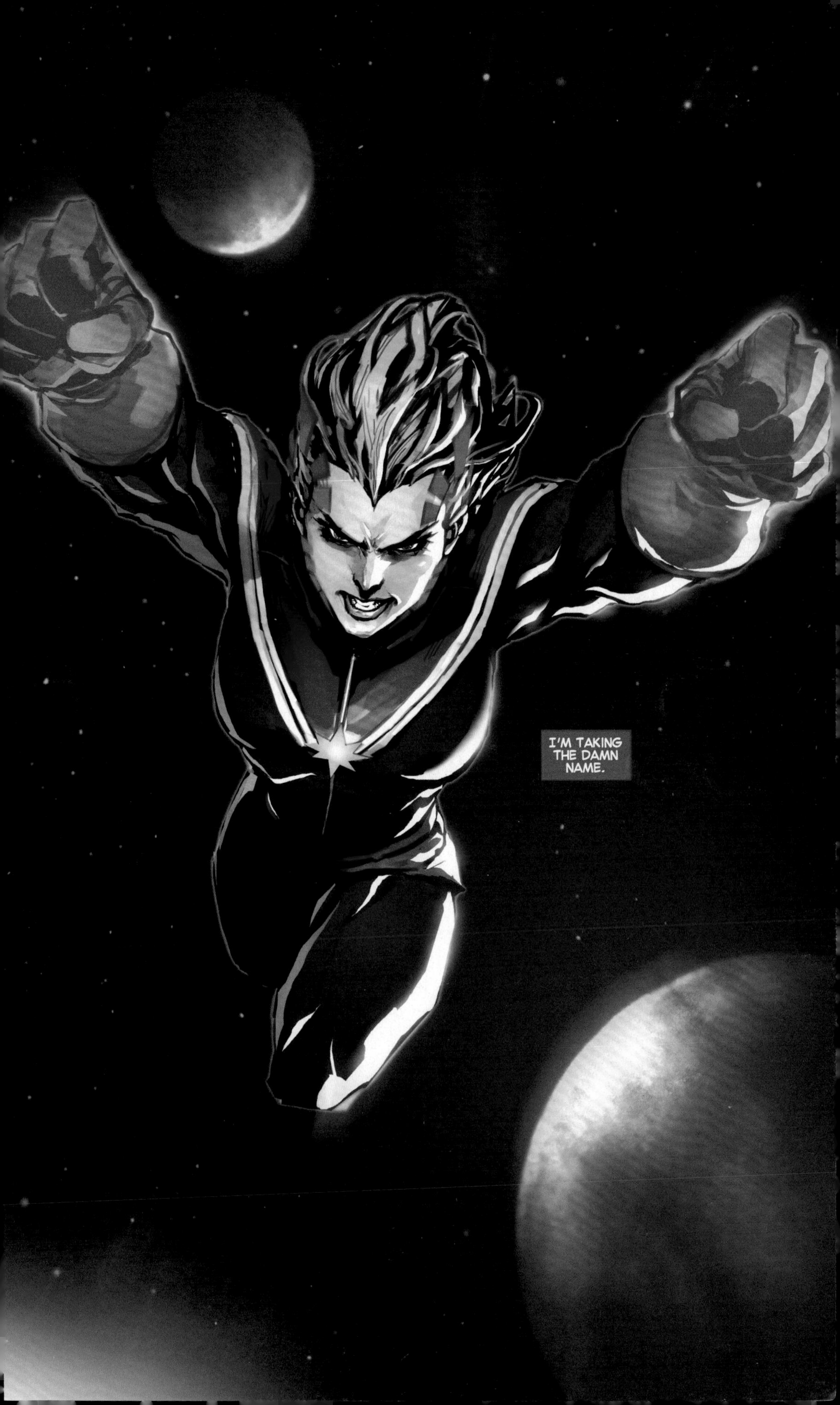
I'M TAKING THE DAMN NAME.

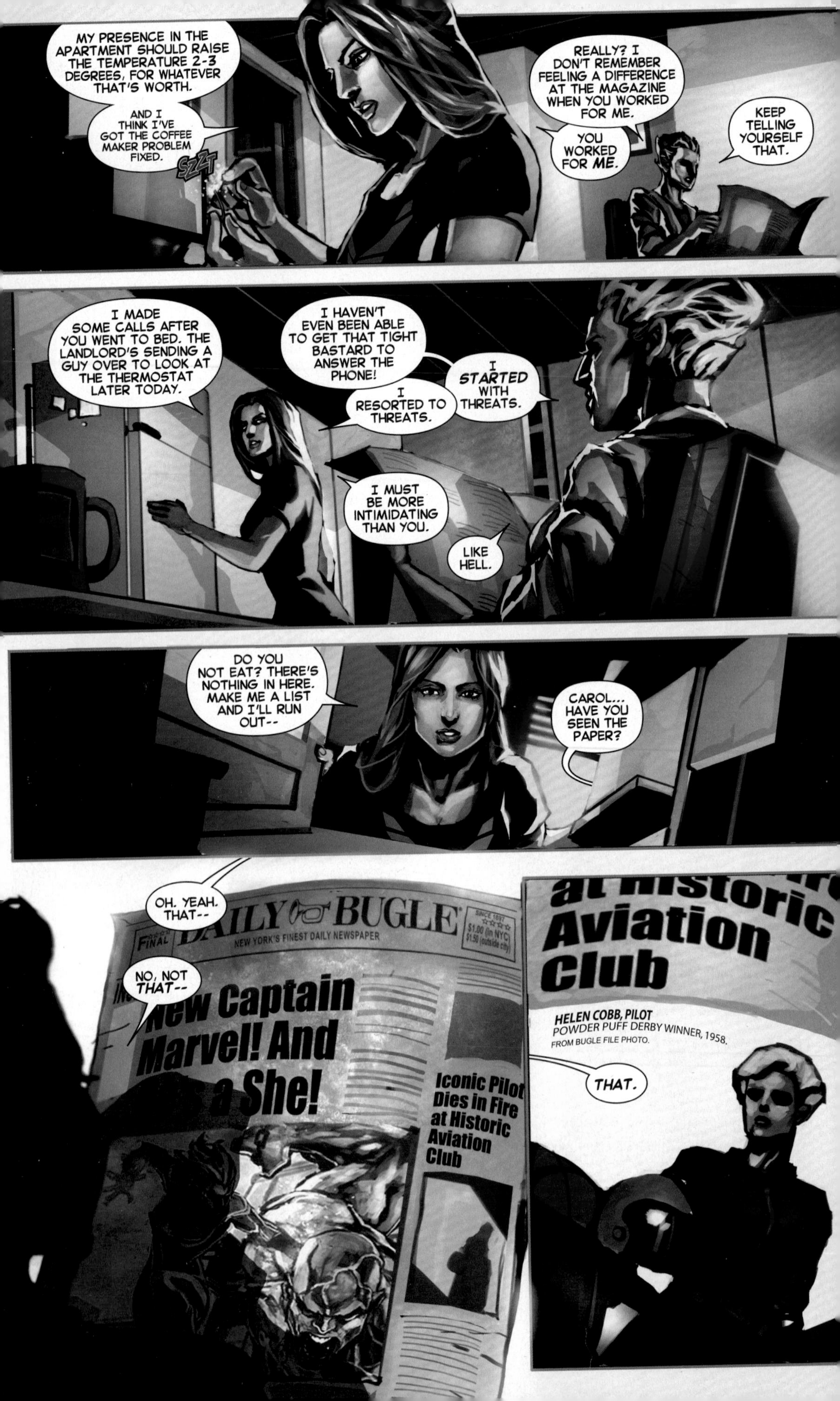

MY PRESENCE IN THE APARTMENT SHOULD RAISE THE TEMPERATURE 2-3 DEGREES, FOR WHATEVER THAT'S WORTH.
AND I THINK I'VE GOT THE COFFEE MAKER PROBLEM FIXED.
SZZT
REALLY? I DON'T REMEMBER FEELING A DIFFERENCE AT THE MAGAZINE WHEN YOU WORKED FOR ME.
YOU WORKED FOR *ME*.
KEEP TELLING YOURSELF THAT.
I MADE SOME CALLS AFTER YOU WENT TO BED. THE LANDLORD'S SENDING A GUY OVER TO LOOK AT THE THERMOSTAT LATER TODAY.
I HAVEN'T EVEN BEEN ABLE TO GET THAT TIGHT BASTARD TO ANSWER THE PHONE!
I *STARTED* WITH THREATS.
I RESORTED TO THREATS.
I MUST BE MORE INTIMIDATING THAN YOU.
LIKE HELL.
DO YOU NOT EAT? THERE'S NOTHING IN HERE. MAKE ME A LIST AND I'LL RUN OUT--
CAROL... HAVE YOU SEEN THE PAPER?
OH. YEAH. THAT--
DAILY BUGLE
FINAL
SINCE 1897
$1.00 (in NYC) $1.50 (outside city)
NEW YORK'S FINEST DAILY NEWSPAPER
NO, NOT *THAT*--
New Captain Marvel! And ... a She!
Iconic Pilot Dies in Fire at Historic Aviation Club
at Historic Aviation Club
HELEN COBB, PILOT
POWDER PUFF DERBY WINNER, 1958.
FROM BUGLE FILE PHOTO.
THAT.

WHY CAN'T I BE SPIDER-MAN? THERE'RE TWO HULKS, TWO CAPS, WHY CAN'T THERE BE TWO--

WE'RE SENDING YOU AFTER TERRORISTS. WE'VE DONE PSYCHE PROFILES. AND TERRORIST AREN'T AFRAID OF SPIDER-MAN.

THEY KNOW HE DOESN'T KILL. VENOM, HOWEVER, WILL KILL YA, EAT YA, AND COME BACK FOR SECONDS.

WE'LL DENY IT, OF COURSE, BUT IT'LL GET OUT-- TO THE RIGHT CIRCLES. AND WHEN IT DOES, THAT'S A NICE REP TO HAVE.

SPEAKING OF THE KILLING...LET ME INTRODUCE YOU TO SOME OF YOUR NEW ORDNANCE...

THIS IS THE MULTI-GUN. SPECIALLY KEYED TO YOUR DNA. IT COST A LOT. DON'T LOSE IT.

KINDA CLUMSY FOR A STANDARD AUTOMATIC.

SHKK

OH!

IT'S ALSO A HIGH-POWERED SNIPER RIFLE.

IT'S A FIREARM FOR EVERY OCCASION.

BUT NEVER FORGET, THAT SUIT--

--THE ALIEN SYMBIOTE, IS YOUR GREATEST WEAPON.

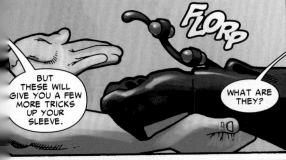

FLORP

BUT THESE WILL GIVE YOU A FEW MORE TRICKS UP YOUR SLEEVE.

WHAT ARE THEY?

KNOCKOUT DRUGS. TRUTH SERUM. AND CHEMICAL WEAPONS OF MY OWN DESIGN.

ALONG WITH VARIOUS KNIVES AND CUTTING TOOLS...

...THE SUIT CAN ALSO FASHION A SYRINGE AS A DELIVERY SYSTEM.

DANG, MACKENZIE. YOU GOT ME HOOKED UP WITH EVERYTHING THIS SIDE OF A SPIDER-SENSE.

YOU'VE GOT SOMETHING BETTER THAN THAT, THOMPSON. YOU'VE GOT ME.

UM... HULLO?

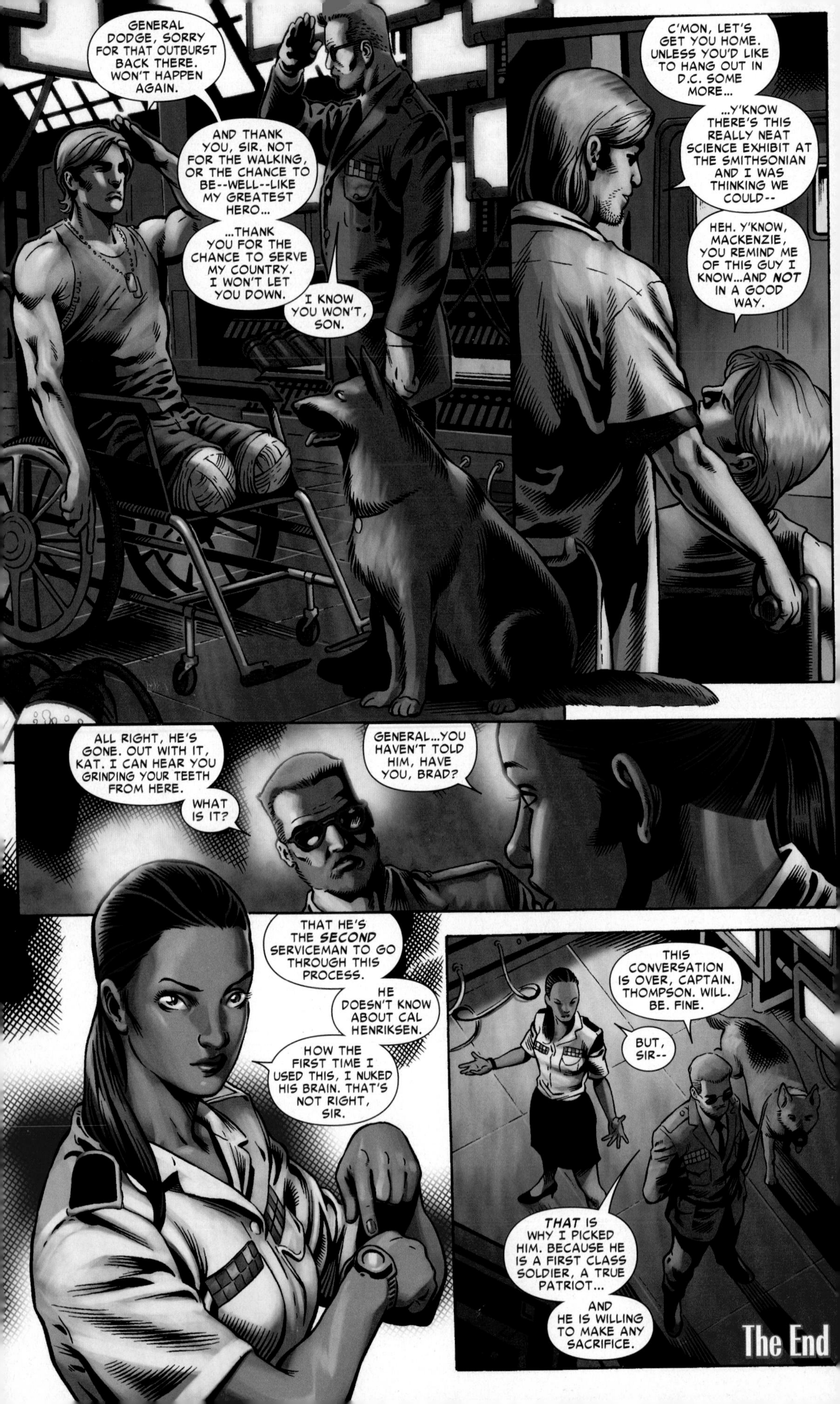
GENERAL DODGE, SORRY FOR THAT OUTBURST BACK THERE. WON'T HAPPEN AGAIN.
AND THANK YOU, SIR. NOT FOR THE WALKING, OR THE CHANCE TO BE--WELL--LIKE MY GREATEST HERO...
...THANK YOU FOR THE CHANCE TO SERVE MY COUNTRY. I WON'T LET YOU DOWN.
I KNOW YOU WON'T, SON.
C'MON, LET'S GET YOU HOME. UNLESS YOU'D LIKE TO HANG OUT IN D.C. SOME MORE...
...Y'KNOW THERE'S THIS REALLY NEAT SCIENCE EXHIBIT AT THE SMITHSONIAN AND I WAS THINKING WE COULD--
HEH. Y'KNOW, MACKENZIE, YOU REMIND ME OF THIS GUY I KNOW...AND *NOT* IN A GOOD WAY.
ALL RIGHT, HE'S GONE. OUT WITH IT, KAT. I CAN HEAR YOU GRINDING YOUR TEETH FROM HERE.
WHAT IS IT?
GENERAL...YOU HAVEN'T TOLD HIM, HAVE YOU, BRAD?
THAT HE'S THE *SECOND* SERVICEMAN TO GO THROUGH THIS PROCESS.
HE DOESN'T KNOW ABOUT CAL HENRIKSEN.
HOW THE FIRST TIME I USED THIS, I NUKED HIS BRAIN. THAT'S NOT RIGHT, SIR.
THIS CONVERSATION IS OVER, CAPTAIN. THOMPSON. WILL. BE. FINE.
BUT, SIR--
THAT IS WHY I PICKED HIM. BECAUSE HE IS A FIRST CLASS SOLDIER, A TRUE PATRIOT...
AND HE IS WILLING TO MAKE ANY SACRIFICE.
The End

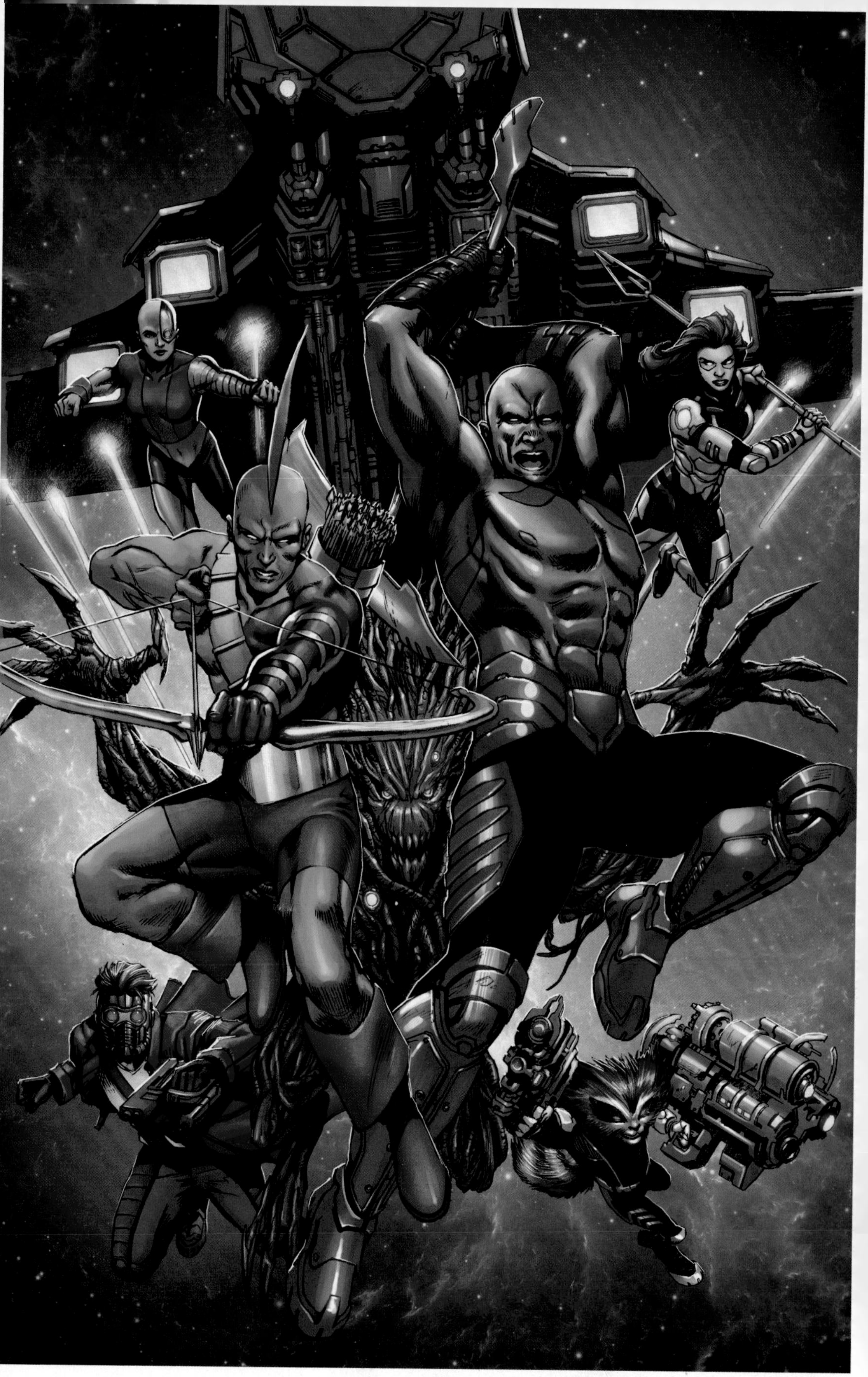

#17 WIZARD WORLD VARIANT
BY ALVARO MARTINEZ & CHRIS SOTOMAYOR

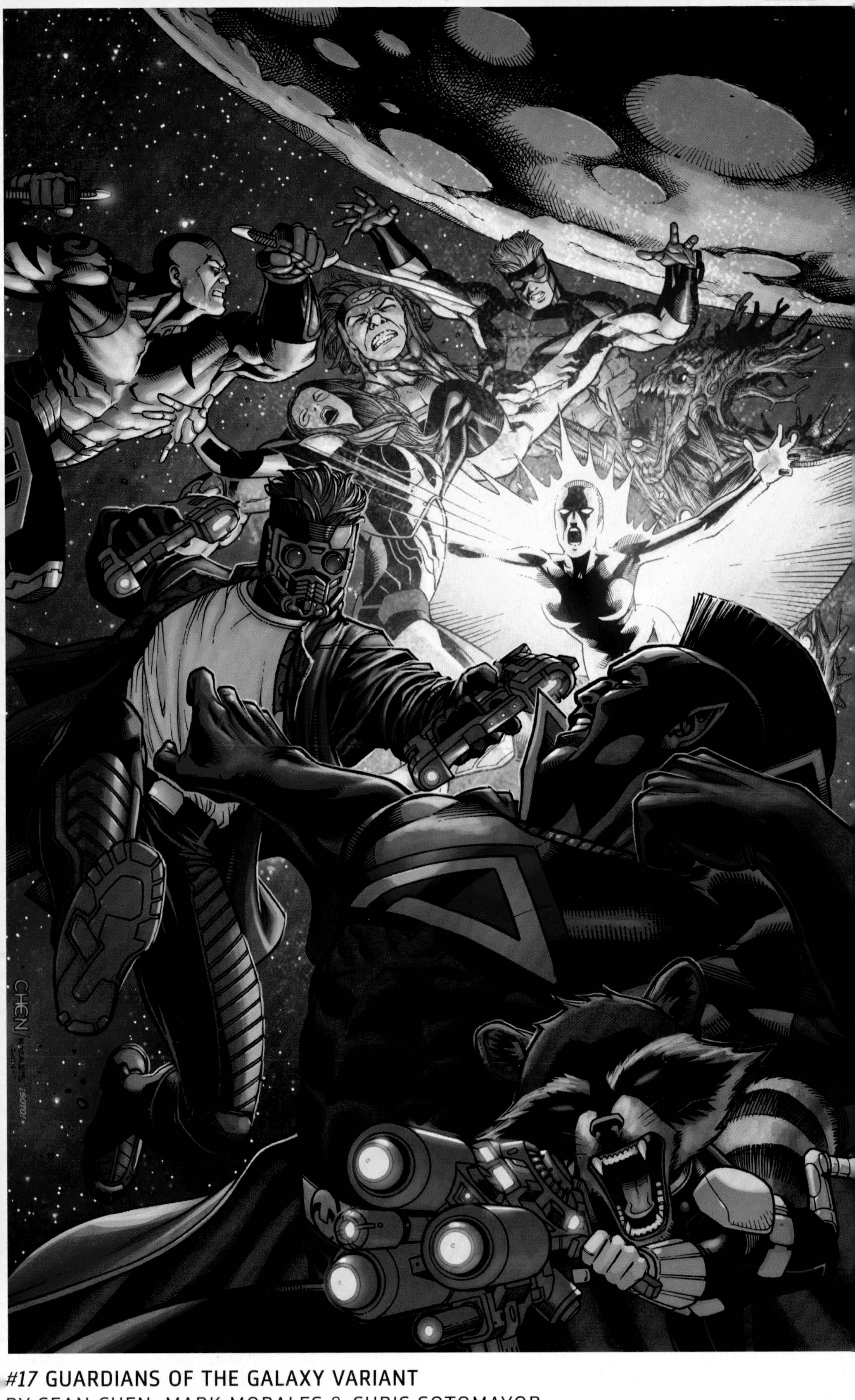
CHEN

#17 GUARDIANS OF THE GALAXY VARIANT
BY SEAN CHEN, MARK MORALES & CHRIS SOTOMAYOR

#17 COVER PENCILS BY ED MCGUINNESS

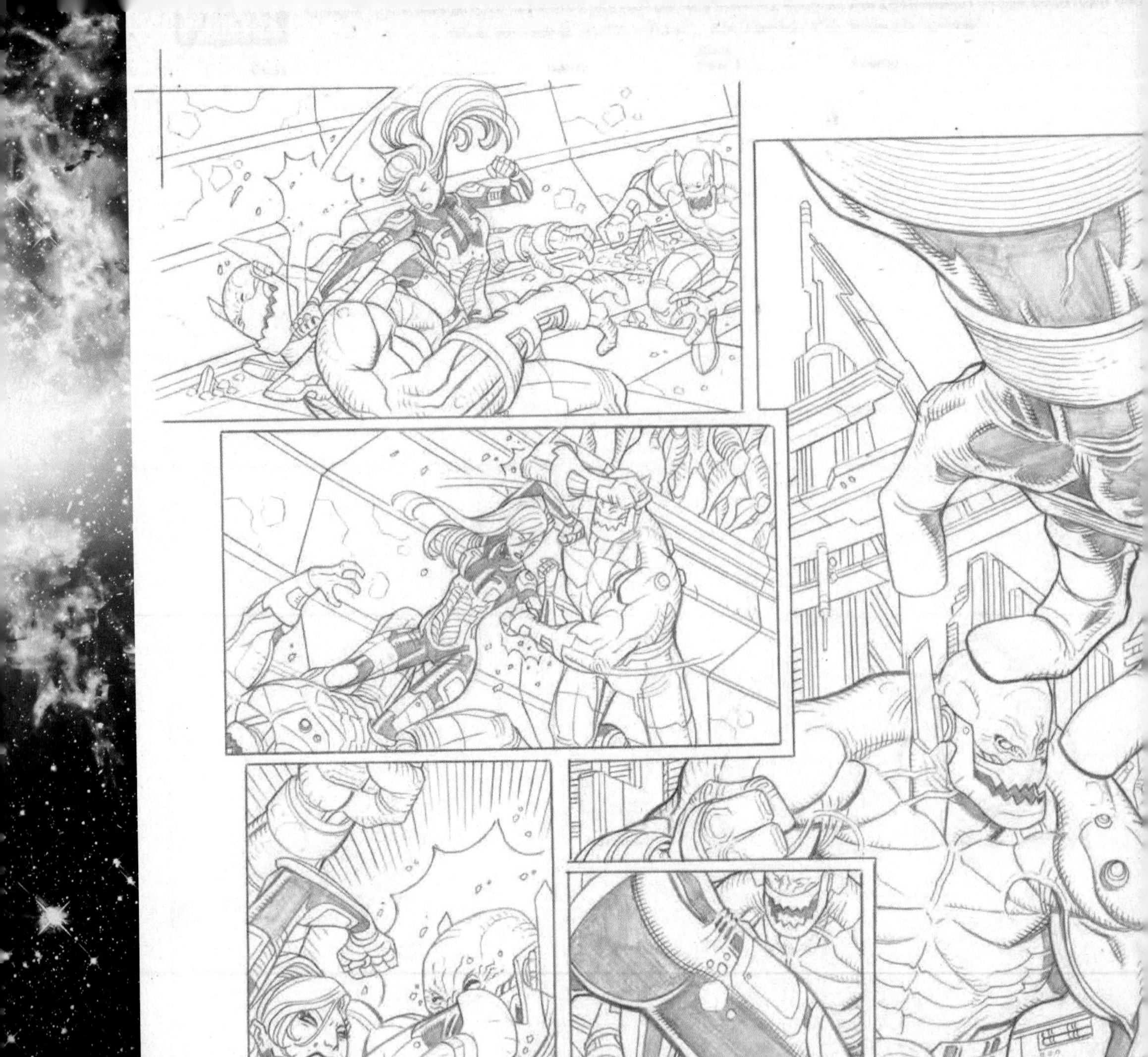

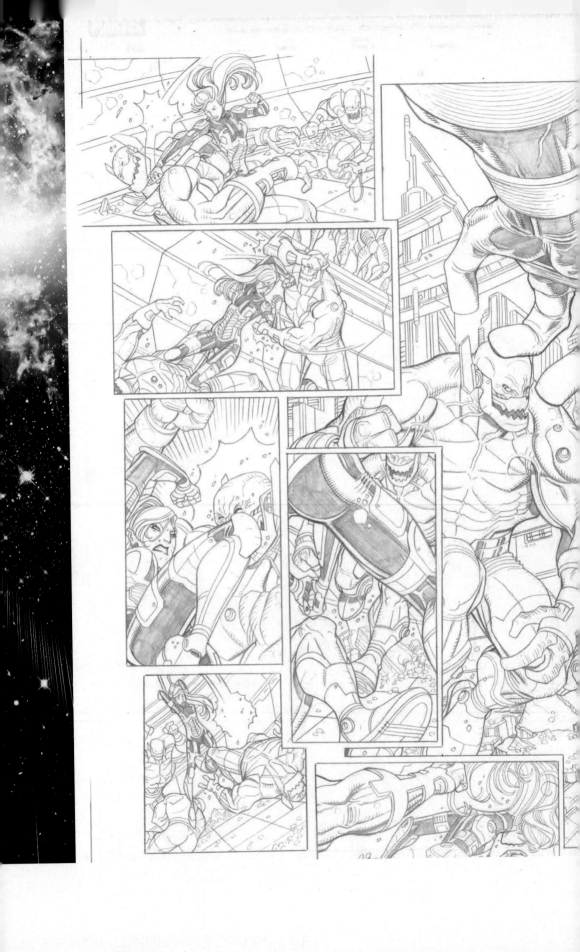

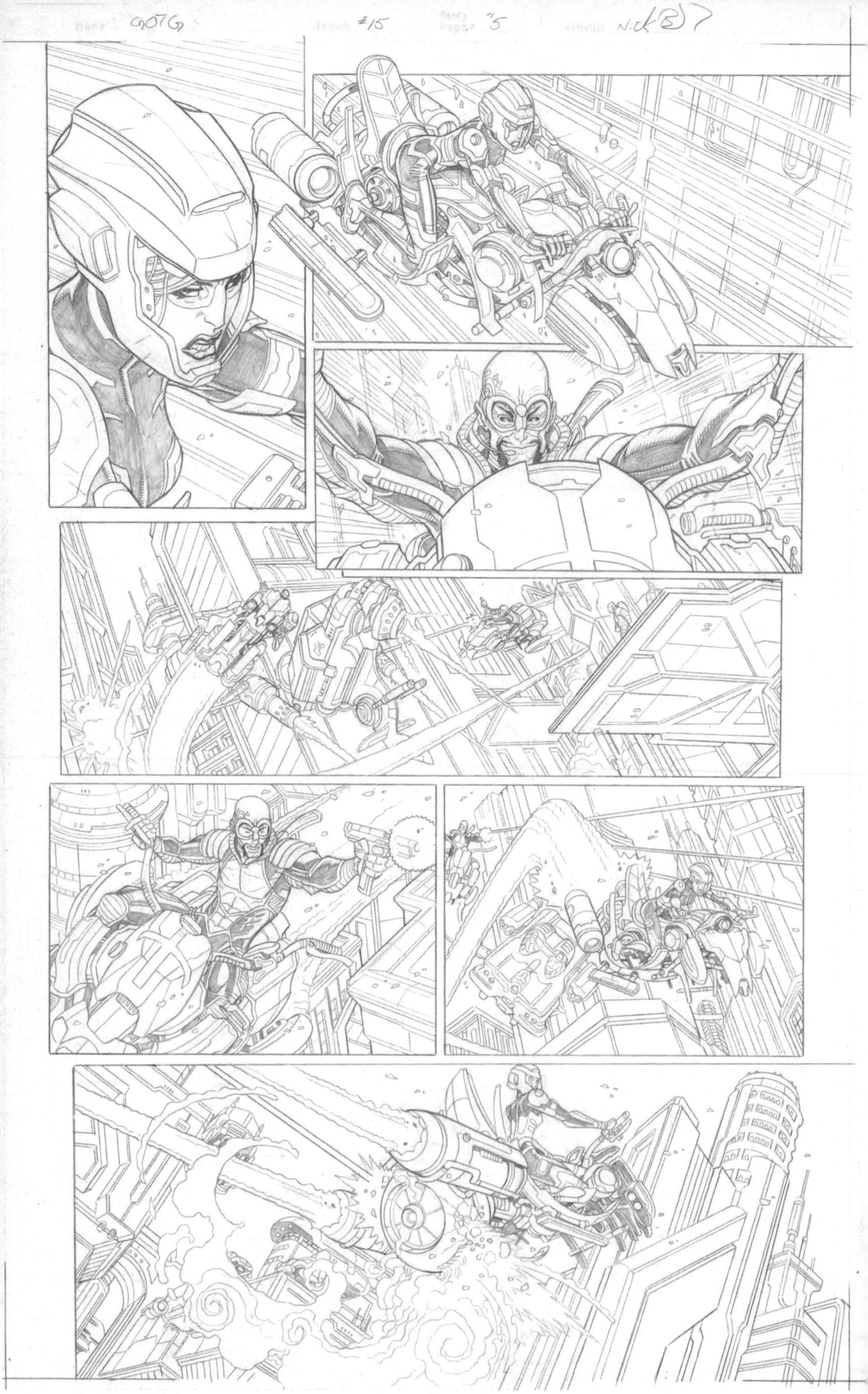

#14, **PAGE 5 PENCILS** BY NICK BRADSHAW

MARVEL AR

AUGMENTED REALITY

MARVEL AUGMENTED REALITY (AR) ENHANCES AND CHANGES THE WAY YOU EXPERIENCE COMICS!

TO ACCESS THE FREE MARVEL AR CONTENT IN THIS BOOK*:

1. Locate the **AR** logo within the comic.
2. Go to Marvel.com/AR in your web browser.
3. Search by series title to find the corresponding AR.
4. Enjoy Marvel AR!

*All AR content that appears in this book has been archived and will be available only at Marvel.com/AR – no longer in the Marvel AR App. Content subject to change and availability.

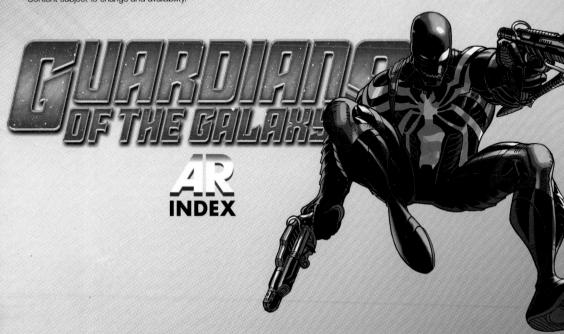

GUARDIANS OF THE GALAXY

AR INDEX